Moon Magic

ROBERT B. RUDDELL
MARTHA SHOGREN
ANNE LIBBY RYLE
Assisted by TANYA HAYES LEE

ALLYN AND BACON, INC.
BOSTON ROCKLEIGH, N.J. ATLANTA DALLAS BELMONT, CALIF.

Acknowledgments

Grateful acknowledgment is made to the publishers, authors, or copyright holders for permission to use and adapt the following materials in this book:

"The Moon's the North Wind's Cooky," reprinted with permission of Macmillan Publishing Co., Inc. from *Collected Poems* by Vachel Lindsay. Copyright 1914 by Macmillan Publishing Co., Inc., renewed 1942 by Elizabeth C. Lindsay.

"The Rabbit in the Moon," adapted from "The Hare in the Moon" by Laura Cathon and Thusnelda Schmidt, from *Perhaps and Perchance: Tales of Nature*. Abingdon, 1962. Taken from *Nature Myths of Many Lands*, American Book Company, © 1910, 1938.

"How High Is the Sky?" from *Sweet As a Pickle and Clean As a Pig* by Carson McCullers. Copyright © 1964 by Carson McCullers and Rolf Gerard. Reprinted by permission of the publisher Houghton Mifflin Company.

"Moon Mouse," from *Moon Mouse*, by Adelaide Holl. Copyright © 1969 by Adelaide Holl. Reprinted by permission of Random House, Inc.

"Squaps, the Moonling," an adaptation of *Squaps, the Moonling* by Ursina Ziegler. Copyright © 1969 by Artemis Verlag, Zurich, Switzerland. English text copyright © 1969 by Atheneum Publishers Inc. Used by permission of Atheneum Publishers.

(continued on page iii)

Cover design: Fujita Design, Inc.

Cover illustration: Robert Byrd

 Library of Congress Catalog Card Number 76-44959

3 4 5 6 7 8 84 83 82 81 80 79 78

"What Is Friendship?" by Carol Aoyagi from *Sounds of Spring.*

"How You Talk," from *How You Talk* by Paul Showers. Copyright © 1966 by Paul Showers, with permission of Thomas Y. Crowell Company, Inc., publisher.

"Sia Lives on Kilimanjaro," adapted with permission of Macmillan Publishing Co., Inc. from *Sia Lives on Kilimanjaro* by Astrid Lindgren. Published in the United States by Macmillan Publishing Co., Inc., 1969.

"The Hen and the Leopard," from *Children's Games from Many Lands* by Nina Millen, copyright Friendship Press, 1943. Used by permission.

"The Something," reprinted with the permission of Farrar, Straus & Giroux, Inc., from *The Something* by Natalie Babbitt. Copyright © 1970 by Natalie Babbitt.

"The Orchard Toy Shop," from *Tops and Whistles* by Carolyn Sherwin Bailey. Copyright 1937 by Carolyn Sherwin Bailey. All rights reserved. Reprinted by permission of The Viking Press, Inc.

"Busy Carpenters," by permission of the author's wife, Mrs. Martha Tippett.

"Take This Hammer," by permission of Hawthorn Books, Inc. from *Take This Hammer* by Sam and Beryl Epstein. Copyright © 1969 by Sam and Beryl Epstein and Tomie de Paola. All rights reserved.

"Pancakes, Pancakes!" adapted by permission of Alfred A. Knopf, Inc. from *Pancakes, Pancakes!* by Eric Carle. Copyright © 1970 by Eric Carle.

"Busy Wheels," adapted by permission of Random House, Inc. from *Busy Wheels,* by Peter Lippman. Copyright © 1973 by Random House, Inc.

"Astronauts and Aquanauts," reprinted from *Have You Seen Houses?,* text © 1973 by Joanne Oppenheim, a Young Scott Book, by permission of Addison-Wesley Publishing Company.

"A Whale," from *The Moon and a Star,* © 1965 by Myra Cohn Livingston. Reprinted by permission of Harcourt Brace Jovanovich, Inc.

"The Dragon Island," from *The Book of Nature Myths* by Florence Holbrook, published by Houghton Mifflin Company, 1902.

"Infinity," from *Just Think!,* by Betty Miles and Joan Blos. Copyright ©1971 by Betty Miles. Reprinted by permission of Alfred A. Knopf, Inc.

"Enuk, My Son," adapted by permission of Pantheon Books, a Division of Random House, Inc. from *Enuk, My Son,* by Claire Fejes. Copyright © 1969 by Claire Fejes.

"I Wonder If Herbie's Home Yet," from *I Wonder If Herbie's Home Yet* by Mildred Kantrowitz. Text copyright © 1971 by Mildred Kantrowitz. By permission of Parents' Magazine Press.

"How the Brazilian Beetles Got Their Beautiful Coats," by Elsie Spicer Eells from *Fairy Tales From Brazil,* published by Dodd, Mead in 1917. By permission of the late author's son, Burr G. Eells, Jr.

"The Bear and the Butterfly," reprinted from *Nibble, Nibble,* text © 1959, by Margaret Wise Brown, a Young Scott Book, by permission of Addison-Wesley Publishing Co.

"The Way of an Ant," copyright © 1970 by Kazue Mizumura from *The Way of an Ant* by Kazue Mizumura with permission of the Thomas Y. Crowell Company, Inc.

"In a Few Words," from *32 Feet of Insides,* by Ronni Solbert. Copyright © 1970 by Ronni Solbert. Reprinted by permission of Pantheon Books, a Division of Random House, Inc.

(continued on page iv)

Illustrations: Analee and Tom Cooke p. 1; Nancy Munger pp. 2-3; Ikki Matsumoto pp. 5-8; Len Ebert p. 9; Lucinda McQueen pp. 10, 12-14, 16-17; John Wallner pp. 18-21, 23-28; Susan Banta pp. 29-30; Analee and Tom Cooke p. 31; Judi Anderson pp. 32-33; Elizabeth Hamlin, Stock Photo p. 32, upper left; Jack Prelutsky, Stock Photo p. 32, lower right; Bobbie Carrey, Stock Photo p. 33, upper left; Frank Siteman, Stock Photo p. 33, lower right; George Ulrich pp. 34-35, 37-38, 40; Monica Anagnostaras pp. 41-42, 44-45, 47-49, 51; Joel Snyder pp. 52-53; Natalie Babbitt pp. 54, 56-61; Lynne Cherry pp. 62, 64, 66-69, 71-73; Leigh Grant pp. 74, 77, 79-80, 82-84, 86; Susan Banta pp. 87-88; Analee and Tom Cooke p. 89; Bill Ogden pp. 90-94, 96-97; True Kelly p. 99; Tom Cooke pp. 100-109; Monica Santa pp. 110-112, 114-118, 120-123; Joe Veno pp. 124-130; Susan Banta pp. 131-132; Analee and Tom Cooke p. 133; Margaret Hathaway pp. 134-135; Cousteau Society, Sea Library p. 136; Ron Church, Tom Stack Associates, pp. 137-138; Mick Church, Sea Library p. 140; Cousteau Society, Sea Library p. 141; C. Roessler, Sea Library p. 142; S. Keiser, Sea Library p. 143; C. C. Wendle, Tom Stack Associates p. 144; Christine Westerberg p. 145; James Watling pp. 146-151; Dave Niles pp. 152-157; Alan Band Associates p. 158; Dave Niles pp. 159-160; Susan Banta pp. 161-162; Analee and Tom Cooke p. 163; Ken Longtemps pp. 164-165; Bernie Colonna pp. 166-168, 171-173; Meryl Henderson pp. 174, 176-183, 185-186; Charles Lilly pp. 187, 189-194, 196, 198-201; Lucinda McQueen pp. 202-204, 206-208, 210-212; Susan Banta pp. 213-214; Analee and Tom Cooke p. 215; Stella Ormai pp. 216-219, 221-222; David McPhail p. 223; Susan Thompson pp. 224-227, 229; Diane Sender p. 230; Bob Dacy pp. 231-234, 237-241; Susan Banta pp. 242-243.

Contents

BUSY HANDS

COME SEE THE SEA

FINDING MY PLACE

TAKE ANOTHER LOOK

Once Upon the Moon

The Moon's the North Wind's Cooky

The Moon's the North Wind's cooky.
He bites it, day by day,
Until there's but a rim of scraps
that crumble all away.

The South Wind is a baker.
He kneads clouds in his den,
And bakes a crisp new moon
  that . . . greedy
North . . . Wind . . . eats . . . again!

—*Vachel Lindsay*

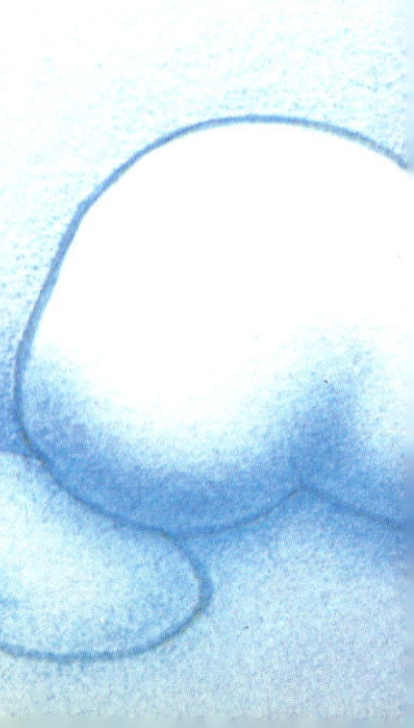

The Rabbit in the Moon

A rabbit, a fox, and a monkey once lived together in India. They wanted to help one another. They were very good friends. They were sure they could live together happily. And they did live happily for many years, helping one another and helping anyone else who was in need.

One day an old man came to their house. "I am very tired and hungry," he said. "May I come into your house and rest for a little while?"

The rabbit, the fox, and the monkey took him into their house. They did everything they could to help him rest.

The man was very pleased with all that they did for him. He sat and talked with them for a long time, asking them about the way they lived together.

By and by he said, "My good friends, you have been so kind to me. May I ask you to do something else for me?

I have been very hungry all day. I tried to hunt, but I didn't catch anything. Can you give me something to eat before I go on my way?"

"We have nothing in the house that a man could eat," said the fox. "But stay here and rest. I will go into the woods and get some food for you."

So the man stayed with the rabbit and the monkey while the fox went out to look for some food.

After some time, the fox came back with a little fruit that he had picked from a tree. He could not find anything else a man could eat.

Then the monkey said, "I will go into the woods and see what I can find."

When he came back, he brought a little more fruit. But he, too, could not find anything else. The hungry man ate the fruit very fast. But there was so little, he was still hungry when it was gone.

Then the rabbit said, "Stay with us a little longer. I will go into the woods and look for food. Maybe I can find more."

The rabbit was gone a long time. He looked and looked, but he could find nothing. At last he came back without anything at all for the man to eat. This made the rabbit very sad. He was a kind little animal and wished to do something for the old man, too.

All at once he said, "Build a fire and I will give you some food."

The man was surprised, but he went out and made a fire near a large rock.

When a good fire was burning, the rabbit went up on the rock. Then he jumped from it into the fire. He would give his meat as food for the old man.

Before the fire touched him,
the old man caught him in his hands.
The old man was really Indra,
the king of all things.

"You have given me a great thing,
dear little rabbit," he cried.
"You have given me yourself.
From now on you shall be my pet.
You will live with me in the sky."

Indra took the rabbit up into the sky
and placed him in the moon. He wanted
everyone on earth to see the rabbit
and to hear the story of his great
kindness and love.

If you look at the spots on the moon,
you can still see the rabbit today.

How High Is the Sky?

The sky is higher than a tree I know.
I know it's higher than an airplane
But when at night there is a starry sky—
I wonder which is higher
Stars or sky?

—*Carson McCullers*

Moon Mouse

by Adelaide Holl

One night, Mother Mouse called to her baby.

"Come, Arthur," she said. "Now that you are old enough, you may stay up after dark. Let us watch the night."

Arthur ran happily to the door of the nest and looked out. The black sky was all around him. Darkness was everywhere.

The night was still and cool.

Arthur felt the coolness on his little nose. It touched his whiskers and his round little ears.

"So this is what the night is like!" he said happily. "It is lovely!"

Arthur looked up. There in the blackness was something big and round and shining.

"Look!" he cried. "Oh, look! Look!"

Mother Mouse smiled.

"It is only the moon," she said. "It is the big, round, yellow moon."

"Where is the moon?" asked Arthur with bright eyes.

"Very far away," his mother told him. "Up, up, high in the sky."

"What is it for?" asked the little mouse.

Mother Mouse said, "It shines in the dark. It gives us light."

"What is it made of?" asked Arthur.

"I do not know," said his mother. "I have heard that it is made of cheese, but I do not think so."

"I would like to go there," said Arthur. "I would like to go to the moon."

His mother smiled. "Well, not tonight," she said. "Come, it is bed time."

Arthur thought about the moon. He thought about it day after day. He thought about it night after night.

"How far away is the moon?" he asked his mother one day.

"Very, very far," she told him. "Farther than the edge of the meadow. Farther than the farmer's corn field. Farther than the fields of golden wheat."

One night, Arthur said to himself, "I am old enough to stay up after dark. I must be old enough to go to the moon."

He looked up. The sky was dark and misty. He could not see the round, yellow moon anywhere.

"I will go look for the moon," said Arthur to himself.

So he set off alone.

He went a long, long way—
past the edge of the meadow,

past the farmer's corn field,
past the fields of golden wheat.

The sky was black and misty.
Then, little by little, the stars began
to come out.

Arthur went on and on until he came
to a place with many lights and
many noises.

And there, all at once, he saw
the moon sitting high on top
of a tall building.

He looked about. He saw steps going up and up and up.

"This must be the way to the moon," he said. So he began to climb.

He climbed until he could go no higher. And there he saw an open place for going in.

"This must be the door to the moon," he said to himself. And in he went.

Sure enough! Inside was something big and round and yellow. And it was made of cheese!

"It is the moon!" cried Arthur, his eyes big and shining.

He ran all about. He ran in and out of the little holes. He nibbled a bit here. He nibbled a bit there. At last, he was very full and very tired.

"The moon is good to eat," he said to himself. "But I think I shall go home now."

He climbed down, all the way down to the ground.

He went a long, long way—
past the fields of golden wheat,
past the farmer's corn field,
past the edge of the meadow.
He went all the way home to his nest.

"Where on earth have you been?" asked Mother Mouse. "I have been looking for you."

"I have been all the way to the moon!" said Arthur. "It is big and round and yellow. It is made of cheese. And it is very good to eat!"

Mother Mouse smiled.

“Funny little mouse!” she said kindly.

Arthur looked up at the night sky. A soft rain was falling. There was darkness all about.

“Where is the moon?” he asked his mother.

“It is a rainy, cloudy night,” she told him. “The moon is hiding.”

Arthur watched for the moon the next night, and again the next. Night after night he watched. But there was only the darkness and the rain.

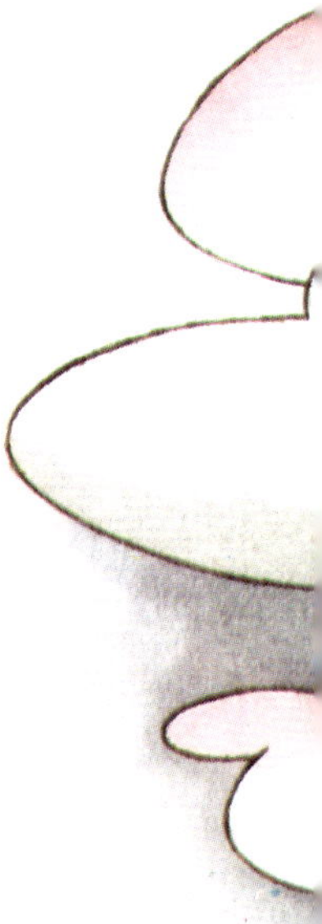

Then one night, the rain stopped.
The clouds began to move away.
All at once, the moon came out.
It was shiny. It was bright.
But it was not big and round.
It was only a small, thin slice.
One whole side was missing.

"Look!" Arthur called to his mother.
"See what a lot of the moon I nibbled!"

"So you did," said his mother
with a smile. "It's a good thing
you did not eat it all up!"

Squaps, the Moonling

by Ursina Ziegler

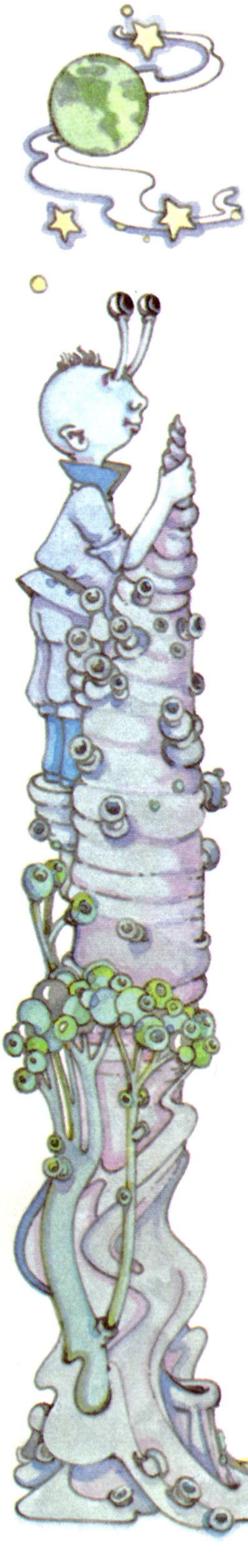

One day an astronaut landed on the moon in his space ship. He came to see if there were any beings on the moon. Most people thought there were not.

The astronaut looked around. The air was still. No sound was heard. There was nothing but sand and stone.

The astronaut wrote in his book, "There is no sign of life on the. . . ."

But someone saw the astronaut. There WAS life on the moon. Little Moonlings were watching him.

Something flew by the astronaut. Was it a bit of dust? He was not sure. It was not dust. It was a Moonling. Moonlings are very interested in new things.

The astronaut looked around. He saw what looked like a pair

of eyes on long stems. The astronaut was surprised. Everything around him seemed to be moving. He closed his eyes. Then he looked again. Everything was still again.

One little Moonling climbed inside the space ship. The astronaut did not see her.

The astronaut finished writing. "There is no sign of life on the moon." He climbed into his space ship and flew home. He came down just on time.

He still did not know
a little Moonling was with him.

Everyone in his home town came to welcome the astronaut. There were people, flowers, and bands. A little girl stepped up to give him flowers. She stopped and looked at his leg.

"Look," she cried. "What's that holding onto your leg? Is it a person or an animal?"

It was the Moonling. She wanted to see the earth. Her eyes on the long stems moved to the right, then to the left. She wanted to see everything around her.

The astronaut remembered the eyes he had seen on the moon. There was life on the moon after all! There were Moonlings! This was one of them. She was so small the astronaut took her home with him. The Moonling would enjoy his three children, Tom, Peter, and Brigitte.

It was very late when the astronaut got home. His children were asleep. He put the Moonling to bed. He covered her up. The Moonling closed her eyes and went to sleep.

Squaps and the Family

The next morning everyone was very excited. Everyone had things to ask the Moonling.

"Tell me, little Moonling, did you really come from the moon?" Peter asked.

"And your necklace, is it made of moon stones?" asked Tom.

"What is your name?" asked Brigitte.

The Moonling looked at them. Then she rubbed her nose, rolled her eyes, and made a face.

"Squaps-pff-krr," she said. This is what Moonlings say when they do not understand.

The children shouted with joy.

"Her name is Squaps. The little Moonling is called Squaps."

Squaps was not her name, but she didn't care. Squaps and Peter and Tom and Brigitte danced around the room. They hid and ran and played games. Squaps soon knew her way around the astronaut's house.

Soon Squaps was out looking around the town. The earth had many new and different things. But Squaps liked it very much.

The best day of all was the day it began to rain. She was playing with the children. There was one drop and then another drop on her head. Squaps was very happy. She had never felt rain before. There was no water on the moon.

Squaps wanted to find out what could be done with water. She wet a cloth and squeezed the water over her head.

Then she took a shower and then a bath. She tipped a watering can over her head. She filled bottles, shoes, hats, and cups. She was very pleased and very happy.

The next day Squaps ran around the garden. She looked at grass and flowers full of morning mist. Brigitte was there, watering the grass with a hose.

"I wish we had a hose like that on the moon," Squaps thought. "What fun the moon children would have playing with water."

Squaps knew that could not be. She played in the water. She ran through it over and over again.

A Party for Squaps

Squaps was happy on Earth. She was even more happy after she found out about water. But sometimes she thought about her home on the moon, and she grew sad. The children tried hard to help her be happy. Squaps still missed the world she knew best.

The children planned a party to cheer her up. It would be a moonlight party on the night of the full moon.

They worked hard. Chairs and tables were set up under the trees. Balloons were hung from the trees. Everyone helped to put out food and drinks.

At eight o'clock on the night of the full moon, the party began. The children took hands. Squaps was in the middle. They danced into the garden.

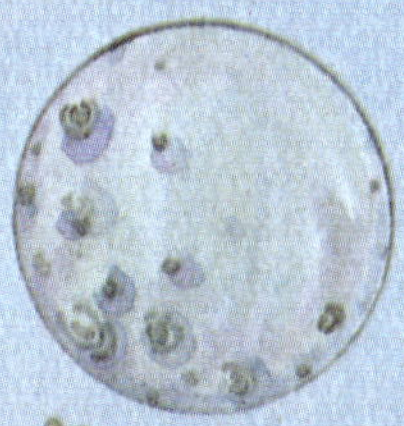

There, high over them, was the full moon. Squaps could not stop looking at it. She felt so strange. She did not know what was wrong with her.

"Pffrr-Krr," came a sound out of nowhere. Squaps found herself floating in the moonlight. She floated higher and higher. She had learned something new. A Moonling

on Earth could fly at the time of the full moon.

The children wanted to try to float, too.

"How do you do it, Squaps?" they asked.

When they tried it, they fell. They looked very silly. Only Moonlings can float on the night of the full moon.

The party went on. There was dancing, playing, and eating. Squaps enjoyed it all. But something seemed to be pulling her and pulling her. Something was pulling her to the moon.

"I must go home," she said to herself. "The earth is nice, but the moon is my home."

The party was over. All the children were asleep. Squaps filled a little bottle with water. She was going to bring it to her friends on the moon.

She left her necklace of moon stones on the table. Then, without a space ship, without a space suit, with only the light of the full moon to make her fly, Squaps went back to the moon.

It was many days before she told everything about the earth. It was the kind of place no one could believe was real. If they had not seen the water, the Moonlings would not have believed it.

Moon Fun

You are on the moon.
You have just met a moonling who says,
"Oo-Hello! Oo-My oo-name oo-is oo-Luna."
Your moon friend means,
"Hello! My name is Luna."
How would you tell Luna your name
in moon talk?

Make these words into moon words.

walk	run	leg
go	duck	bed

Can you say something else to Luna
in moon talk?

Make a Pair

Stories happen in different places. When we read a story, we can find out where it takes place. Read each story below. Then look at the pictures. Tell which picture goes with each story. How did you know?

Mary loved the trees and water. Her long dress got wet as she put a toe in the water.

Mary looked around. There was no life at all. Her space boots stepped in the dust.

Mary looked down. The trees below looked like small dots. She was moving fast.

Mary's arms hung down from the bars. It was funny to see the world upside down.

Talking Together

What Is Friendship?

Wendy
Big nose.
Very long hair.
Her eyes are black.
Friend.

—Yvonne Mui

Yvonne
Small, nice
thin, naughty, short
laughing, crying, running, playing
friend.

—Wendy Gee

Friends.
Happy, nice
good and fun.
Friends are very good
buddies.

—Mark Bayless

Friends.
They're good.
They are funny.
They make me sad.
Happy.

—Emanuel Rutledge

Friendship.
Being nice.
Happy, joyful, playing.
Exciting, full of joy.
Friends.

—Iona Mahtab

How You Talk

by Paul Showers

Have you wondered how you make sounds when you talk? How DO you talk to your family and friends?

Let's try something.

Stand up and put your hands on your chest. Feel your ribs with your fingers. Inside your ribs are your lungs. Close your mouth, and take a deep breath. As your breath goes into your lungs, your chest gets bigger.

Air goes in your nose, down through your throat, and into your lungs. Take in as much air as you can. Now say Ahhhhhhhhh, and let the air out s-l-o-w-l-y. Say Ahhhhhh as long as you can. When you run out of air, you run out of Ahhhhhh. You use your lungs when you talk.

Take another deep breath. Put your head back, and feel your throat with your fingers. Let out your breath again and say Ahhhhhhhhh.

Can you feel the place in your throat where the sound is made?

The place where the sound is made is called the *larynx*. Sometimes it is called your voice box. It is a place in your throat where air goes through a very small opening. Air goes down through the larynx when your breath goes in, and up through the larynx when your breath goes out.

You can take a breath in and let it out without making a sound. But when you want to talk or sing, then you use your larynx.

Let's try something else.
Get a balloon and make believe the neck of the balloon is your throat. Blow up the balloon.

Hold the neck of the balloon shut with both hands. Pull the opening of the balloon until it makes a thin slit.

As the air comes through the slit, it makes a strange sound. If the slit is very thin, the sound is high.

As the slit opens, the sound goes lower.

Your larynx works something like the slit in the balloon.

But your larynx works much better. You can use it to make ALL KINDS OF SOUNDS.

Hold a mirror up to your mouth. Curl back your lips and show your teeth. Open your mouth and stick out your tongue. Tap your upper teeth with the end of your tongue.

Close your mouth and hum.
Keep on humming and hold the end of your nose shut with your fingers. Let go. Hold it shut again. Say, "My, my, my," and "No, no, no," and "Sing, sing, sing."

You use your nose when you hum. You use it when you make the sounds for *m* and *n* and *ng*.

Watch your mouth in the mirror, and make these sounds:

Ma-ah-ah-ah
Me-ee-ee-ee
Moo-oo-oo-oo.

You make different sounds as you move your mouth. When you talk you use your lungs, your larynx, your mouth, your nose, your lips, your tongue, and your teeth.

How do you use your lips? Look in the mirror and say, "Beans and bananas, bottles and birds." Say it again slowly and watch your lips. Can you say these sounds without using your lips? TRY IT.

Open your mouth wide. Watch your lips in the mirror. Keep them open wide. Don't let your lips touch. Now say, "Beans and bananas." Say, "Bottles and birds." Can you do it?

You use your tongue for other sounds. Try this.

Open your mouth and hold down your tongue with a spoon.

Say, "Rabbits and rainbows, rooms and rope."

Say, "Ladders and lions, leaves and lace."

You use your teeth when you talk. Open your mouth. Look in the mirror and say, "Think, thin, and three." Watch how your tongue touches your teeth. Say, "This, that, these, and they."

People use many kinds of sounds when they talk. It takes a long time to learn how to make these sounds. You should never laugh at anyone who cannot make the sounds well. You had to learn them, too.

Sia Lives on Kilimanjaro

by Astrid Lindgren

Kilimanjaro is the name of a mountain. It is very high. It is one of the most beautiful mountains in the whole world. Kilimanjaro is in Africa.

Sia is a little girl who lives on Kilimanjaro. She does not live at the top. The top is covered with snow. Sia lives down near the bottom. She lives near the banana trees and the coffee bushes.

Sia and her brother Sariko live in a hut with a straw roof. There are no windows, only an opening for a door. Her mother and father and small brothers and sisters live there, too. They belong to the Chagga people.

Sia is only eight years old, but she can already help with the work. She cuts grass for the animals with a grass knife. Her little sister Linga wants to learn how to cut grass, too. SHE is too little, only six.

Linga CAN help carry the grass home on her head.

Sia's small brothers, Saika and Kitutu, want to be with Sia all the time.

"But I can't carry both of you at the same time," says Sia.

She gives Kitutu a box.

"Here, Kitutu," she says, "you can make believe this is a boat."

"It's not a boat," says Kitutu, "it's a car."

Sia and Sariko love their kind, happy father.

"What do you think Mother and I are going to do tomorrow?" asks Sia's father. "We are going to the Chagga Feast at Moshi to see King Marealle."

"I want to go with you," says Sariko.

"I do, too," says Sia.

"But who will look after little Saika then?" her mother asks. "Who will make Kitutu be good?"

"Aunt Mamole," Sia says.

"No, you are too young to go to the feast," says her father. "Children must stay home."

The next morning Mother and Father set out for Moshi.

"Goodbye. Look after the little ones! Don't let Linga play with the grass knife. See that Kitutu doesn't get lost," they say.

Sia cried a little. She DID want to go to the feast.

"YOU see that Kitutu doesn't get lost," says Sariko. "You are too small to see the king and the chiefs, Sia, but I'm not. I'm going to Moshi."

And then Sariko ran off by himself.

"If he can go, I can, too," thinks Sia. "I'll follow him."

Sariko does not see Sia coming behind him.

"Aunt Mamole can look after the babies. I will go to Moshi to see King Marealle," says Sia.

On the way, Sariko sees elephants and other animals, but he doesn't see Sia. She is too small.

Someone is building a hut in the middle of the forest. It is Kifura, a friend of Sariko and his family.

"Get me a bunch of bananas," says Kifura, "and take one or two for yourself."

Sariko uses a long pole with a knife at the end to cut the bananas.

After some lunch, Sariko starts on his way again. Then he hears something behind him.

He hears a tiny laugh. There is Sia.

"Sariko, I am not too young to go to look at kings and chiefs," says Sia.

Sariko is very angry.

"Go home," he says, "go home to Aunt Mamole and the babies. Only big children may go

to the Chagga Feast. It's a long way to Moshi. How will you get there? You can't walk. I'm going to get a ride in a car."

Here comes a truck, just as Sariko stops talking. Sariko waves at the driver and asks for a ride.

"Climb up behind," says the driver. "You will be in Moshi in no time at all."

Sariko leaves Sia standing by the road.

"If he can ride, so can I," thinks Sia. "There will be more cars. If only I can ask for a ride!"

"Please will you give me a ride?"

There are lots of cars on the way to Moshi today. Even though Sia does not ask out loud, the drivers know what she wants. In no time at all she is in Moshi, too.

There are big children everywhere in Moshi.

"What if Sariko was right? Maybe little children cannot go to the Chagga Feast," thinks Sia. She is a little frightened, but she is glad she came.

"Well, I'm here, and while I'm here, I'll see what I can see," thinks Sia. "Where is King Marealle?"

Sia sees him! She thinks he looks like a fine king. He looks very kind, also.

"He will not mind if I speak to him."

"Good morning," says Sia.

"Hello, hello!" says King Marealle. "And who are you?"

"My name is Sia," she says.

"I have come a long way to see you."

"Over there is Sariko," says Sia. She points her finger at her brother.

"He said I was too small to look at kings and chiefs, but I'm not."

"No, not at all," says King Marealle. "Maybe I should talk to Sariko, too."

Sia's mother and father are standing with the people who have come to see the king.

"I must be dreaming," says Sia's mother. "It can't be Sia and Sariko talking to the king."

"I don't understand," says Father. "We must have a word with them when we get home."

"But just think! OUR children have spoken to King Marealle," says Mother. "We will not be too cross. They are small, but they have done something very big."

The Chagga Feast is over. Sia is tired. She is glad to go home in a car with Sariko.

"I am not too small to look at kings and chiefs," says Sia.

"No, Sia, I see you aren't," says Sariko. "You are as big as Kilimanjaro."

The Hen and the Leopard

by Nina Millen

Sia and Sariko play many games with their friends. Some are like games played in the United States.

Here is a game played in many parts of Africa. Sometimes it is called, "The Hen and the Wildcat." Sometimes it is called "The Hen and the Leopard." In the United States, it is called "Fox and Geese." Its African name is "Ngale Kup Ba Ze."

"The Hen and the Leopard" game may be played inside or outside.

One player is the Mother Hen. One player is the Leopard who growls and tries to catch the chickens. All the other players are chickens. To make the game more fun, there should be six chickens or more.

The chickens get in line behind the Mother Hen. Each chicken

holds the next player at the waist.

The Leopard stands in front of the line. It moves its body as if dancing and growls softly.

The Mother Hen sings in a chanting voice, "The Leopard comes to catch you!"

The chickens chant back, "Poor children! Poor children!"

With a growl, the Leopard tries to catch a chicken. Quickly, the chickens fall to the ground.

If the Leopard catches a chicken before it falls, the chicken must leave the game.

The game starts again. It goes on until all the chickens are caught.

The Something

by Natalie Babbitt

The truth is that Mylo was very much afraid of the dark. When his mother asked him why, he had a hard time answering.

Finally he said, "I keep thinking something will come in through the window."

"What kind of a something?" asked Mylo's mother. "Robbers, I suppose? Or ghosts? There's no such thing as ghosts, you know. And even if we had some robbers, they wouldn't be interested in you."

And Mylo's mother, who liked to explain things, went on to tell about the habits and customs of robbers.

"I'm not worried about robbers," said Mylo, though he did hate to disappoint her. "And it's not ghosts either."

"Well, what is it then?" said Mylo's mother.

"Just a Something," said Mylo.

This left his mother with nothing at all to explain. She felt very bad about not being able to help him. So the next day she went out and bought a large package of modeling clay and gave it to him and that made her feel better.

Mylo didn't know what to do with the clay at first. Mostly he made lumps and thumb prints. Or rolled it into snakes.

But after a while he found himself trying to make a statue of the Something he was afraid of in the night.

Every day he worked with the clay. And every day he learned a little more about how to make it do what he wanted.

Mylo's mother explained to her friends, "I didn't realize how artistic Mylo is," she said. "He's so busy with his clay, he's forgotten all about being afraid of the dark."

But the real reason why Mylo was so quiet at night was this: He was trying to figure out exactly what the Something looked like. He found himself almost wishing it WOULD come in through the window so he could get a good look at it and make a better statue in the morning.

Mylo Has a Dream

Then one day everything seemed to go just right, and suddenly there it was. He had made a perfect statue of the Something. He was very proud of his work.

When he showed it to his mother, she said, "That's beautiful, Mylo," in such a special voice that he knew she had no idea what it was.

But it didn't matter. Mylo didn't try to explain. He carried the statue to his room and put it on the table by his bed.

That night Mylo went right to sleep and dreamed he was wandering out in the wild dark. He came to a sort of window, and all at once, the Something was there, climbing through.

It was the very Something he had modeled out of clay. But he found he wasn't afraid any more.

He spoke right up to it. "Hello," he said. "My name is Mylo and I'm not afraid of you at all."

"I'm not afraid of you either," said the Something. "But I wish you'd get out of my dream."

"This isn't your dream," said Mylo. "This is my dream. And anyway, I was just leaving."

"Goodbye then," said the Something. "It was nice talking to you."

And then Mylo woke up.

In the morning his mother said, "Aren't you going to play with your clay today?"

"No," said Mylo. "I'm tired of it now."

But he kept the statue of the Something for a long time afterward. He kept it because he was the only one who knew what it was. And he didn't want to forget too quickly.

Thief in the Hall

by Linda Hirschmann

"Here, Lucky!" Jeff held out the stick. "Jump over."

Jasmine smiled. She knew what would happen.

Lucky jumped, grabbed the stick in his mouth, and ran away.

Jasmine laughed.

"You'll see," Jeff said. "I'll train him yet."

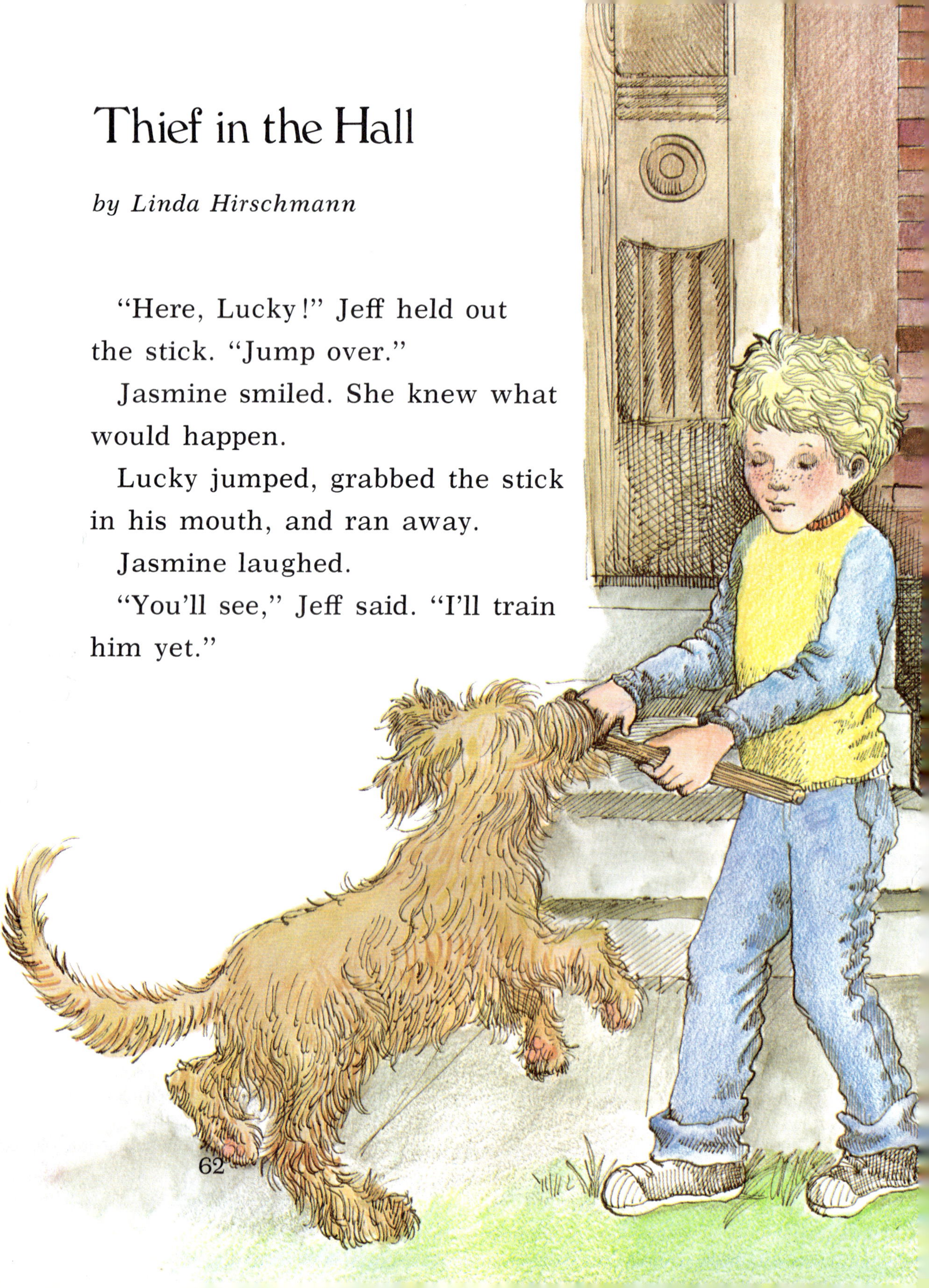

"All I can see is how well Lucky has trained you," said Jasmine. "He wants a stick to run away with, and you give him one."

Jeff shook his head. "People train dogs, Jasmine. Dogs don't train people."

Jasmine went inside and opened the door to her apartment. It was quiet. Jasmine was always the first one home. Her sister Mai Ling was still in school. Their parents were at work.

Jasmine pulled out the vacuum cleaner. On Wednesday, vacuum. That was her mother's rule. Jasmine didn't mind. She thought of the vacuum cleaner as an animal that ate dirt. She enjoyed feeding it.

She worked quickly. She always did when her mother wasn't there to say, "Don't forget to dust under the chairs." She had just finished when someone knocked on the door.

Jeff's sister, Peggy, was in the hall.

"Have you seen my doll Susan?" Peggy asked.

"Of course, I've seen her, " Jasmine told her. "Don't you remember you let me play with her yesterday? She's very pretty."

Peggy stomped her foot. "No, no! Have you SEEN her TODAY, NOW? She's missing. Where did you leave her?"

"Is she lost?" Jasmine asked.

"I left her next to your door last night just as you told me to."

"You didn't," said Peggy. "I looked there last night, but she wasn't there. I want my doll. Now!"

"Where do you think she could be?" asked Jasmine. "I'll help you look."

"I know where she is," Peggy answered. "YOU have her."

"Oh, no! I don't have her. I put her by the door."

"Thief!" Peggy yelled. "I'll tell Mother. I'll tell Jeff."

She ran to her apartment.

Jasmine began to cry. She was still crying when Mai Ling came home.

"I didn't take it," she told her sister.

"I know that," Mai Ling said. "Don't cry. Peggy will find her doll. Don't worry."

But Jasmine did worry. She worried all afternoon, and she was still worrying at dinner.

"You're so quiet, Jasmine. Are you all right?" her mother asked.

"I'm all right," Jasmine answered. "But I'm worried about Peggy's doll. It's lost."

Jasmine told her parents that the doll was lost. But she couldn't tell them Peggy called her a thief.

"Thief!" A woman yelled in the hall. "Thief!"

Jasmine dropped her bowl. The woman was Peggy's mother. Did she think Jasmine was a thief, too?

She looked at Mai Ling. They ran into the hall.

People ran out of every apartment.

"My purse is gone," Mrs. Brown told them. "I was almost out the door when the phone rang. I went back to answer it. I sat in the chair with my purse on the floor next to me. When I hung up, it was gone."

"You left the hall door open?" a man asked.

"Yes," Mrs. Brown said. "Someone came in and out again while my back was turned. Who could do such a thing?"

Peggy looked right at Jasmine.

Jasmine Finds a Fork

After school the next day, Jasmine walked home quickly. She didn't speak to anyone. When she got home, she didn't do her work. She didn't even touch the bowl of fruit on the table. She just sat and did nothing. She thought about Peggy and the doll and the purse.

Then she heard the garbage truck. She went to the window to watch it.

"It sounds like a hungry stomach, but much louder than ours could ever be," she thought. "It's as loud as a dragon's stomach."

She thought about the Chinese New Year's dragon eating garbage. It made her laugh for the first time that day.

Just then something fell from a garbage can. It shined in the sunlight. She saw Lucky jump for it. Then he ran away.

"That Lucky! He thinks the garbage truck is playing with him," laughed Jasmine.

Suddenly she had an idea. Quickly she ran downstairs.

Lucky was gone when she reached the street, but she knew where he would go. He had something to bury, so he would go to the nearest spot of dirt.

She found him there, digging. An old fork, bent but still shiny, lay next to him. Jasmine picked it up.

Lucky growled at her, and she gave it back.

Jasmine dug next to Lucky in the soft dirt. When her hand hit something hard, she pulled it out. It was a bone.

"Here, boy. Catch!"

She tossed the bone. Lucky jumped up and grabbed it. Away he ran.

Jasmine kept digging. Again her hand hit something. This wasn't another bone. It was soft, like cloth. She dug out more dirt.

"Mrs. Brown's purse! Oh, Lucky! You did take it!" she cried.

She jumped up with the purse and raced for home. Then she stopped. She turned around and hurried back to the dirt. She dug quickly. In one hole she found another bone. In a second hole, there was nothing. In the next hole, Jasmine found what she was looking for. The doll!

Jasmine ran into the apartment house.

"Mai Ling! Peggy! Jeff! Mrs. Brown!" she shouted.

They met her in the hall.

"Look! Lucky took them. He buried them," said Jasmine.

Peggy looked at her. "I don't believe you," she said. "You took them. Now you're saying Lucky did it."

Jasmine didn't know what to say. She dropped the doll and the purse. She turned to leave.

Just then, Lucky ran in, his tail moving fast. He looked at Peggy and Mrs. Brown. Then he saw the doll. Before anyone could stop him, he picked it up in his mouth and ran.

Peggy caught him as he reached the stairs.

"Lucky!" she cried. "Bad dog!"

She took her doll away from Lucky. Then she turned and looked at Jasmine.

"I'm sorry," she said in a low voice. "I'm sorry I called you a thief."

Jasmine didn't answer.

Peggy was very unhappy. She wanted Jasmine to know how sorry she was. She tried to think of a way to show her. She held out the doll.

"Would you like to play with Susan?" she asked.

Jasmine looked away.

"What can I do?" Peggy wondered. Then she walked over to Mai Ling and whispered into her ear. Mai Ling whispered back.

"Dor jeh," Peggy said.

Jasmine looked up in surprise. "You're welcome," she said quietly.

Mai Ling whispered to Peggy again.

"Ho dor jeh," Peggy said.

Jasmine laughed. "And you're welcome very much," she answered.

Happy Birthday

by Dolly Hasinbiller

Suzie looked at the bicycle on the ground. Then she looked at her knee. There was a big new scrape on top of her old scrape. It hurt.

She got up slowly. She looked at the big black bike. It was bigger than she was. She pushed and pulled. Finally, she got it up.

Suzie was covered with scrapes. Every night, when she went to bed, she found new ones. Last night there were six new scrapes. There would be even more tonight.

She had been on the bike every day that week. Riding a bike didn't look that hard. Just about all her friends could ride a two wheeler. Her brothers, Clem and Jeff, had been riding bikes for a long time. But they were BIG! If only her legs were long, the way Clem's were.

Suzie had found Jeff's old bike in the barn. She was learning to ride on it. But it was hard! Sometimes she wished the bike had six wheels. Sometimes she even thought she would give up on bicycles and learn to drive a car. She would drive over the farm in the truck, waving at Clem and Jeff on their bikes.

Nobody in Suzie's family knew that she was learning to ride a bike.

It was her secret. Her birthday would come soon. They would give her a new bike. She would walk up to it, get on, and ride off! Suzie smiled as she thought of Jeff and Clem just standing there, watching her. They never thought she could do anything.

Suzie hurt all over from falling off the bike so much. Now her knee hurt from the new scrape. She thought she had better cover it up. She did not want anyone to know. She was surprised nobody had seen the scrapes.

Everybody was pretty busy, though. There was a lot of work to do on the farm this late in summer. Grandmother was canning tomatoes and other things from the garden. Clem and Jeff were helping her. Their father was busy all day outdoors. At night, he was in the kitchen, cooking dinner. Suzie had been left pretty much alone.

That night at dinner, her father said, "Well Suzie, do you still want that bike for your birthday?"

Clem spoke up. "She's too little to ride a two wheeler," he said. "Look at those legs. How would she even get on a bike?"

Jeff laughed. "That's right. And if she did get on, she'd fall off and land on her head." He made a face at her.

"Will you please let Suzie talk," said their grandmother.

"Thank you," said Suzie. She sat up in her chair and looked her father in the eye. "I do want a bicycle for my birthday," she said. "And that is the only thing I want."

"OK" said her father. "That's it. You want a bicycle for your birthday."

"It has to be red," Suzie told her father. "Red is the only kind I want."

The next morning, Suzie was out before the sun. She got the old bike up the hill to the barn and held it up with the kickstand. Then she fixed the pedal. The pedal had to be in the right place when she got on. Then she could get her foot just right. The hill helped, too. She put an old box by the bike. Everything was ready.

Suzie held the bike with one hand. She put up the kickstand with the other hand. She got up on the box. Then, with her left leg still on the box, she jumped.

Up went her left leg. Down went her right foot on the pedal. And away went Suzie!

Not for long, though. After about a meter, the bike began to tip. Suzie kept pedaling, but it was too late. This time she jumped out of the way before the bike fell on her. "My riding is no good," she thought, "but my falling is doing a lot better."

All morning was like that. Every time she went a meter or so, the bike began to fall. But Suzie kept trying. One time she tried sitting up taller when the bike began to tip. That time, she fell on the bike. Nothing worked. Suzie gave up for the day. That night, she didn't even look at her scrapes.

The next day, she didn't do much better. But the day after that, Suzie went about two meters before she fell off. By lunch time, she

could go three meters. It was going to work, after all! And just in time, too. Her birthday was three days away.

The next day, Suzie got up and ran to the window. It was raining! "Oh, no," she thought. "That's all I need. I'll never learn to ride in time, now, never!" It rained all day.

That night at dinner, Suzie was very sad. "Look at that face," said Clem. "Look at the face on our little sister. It looks as if it got left out in the rain."

"Dad must have told her the store was all out of red bikes," said Jeff.

"What?" cried Suzie, jumping up from her chair. "But I said red is the only color I want."

Clem and Jeff laughed. "He got you that time," said Clem.

"Well, I got her to talk," said Jeff.

Suzie looked at Jeff. Then she looked at Clem. "You are in for a very big surprise," she said.

"When you see me on that bicycle . . ." She stopped. Then she ran out of the room.

"You on a bicycle?" Jeff called. "It'll be a surprise, all right."

The next day turned out to be the best day Suzie had. Riding the bike was getting better all the time. She could make it down the hill without falling off. She even turned a few times. Sometimes she fell down when she turned, but sometimes she didn't. It was looking as if Suzie could do it.

The morning of her birthday, Suzie went into the kitchen. Her grandmother was making her a cheeseburger. That was because birthday people in her family could have anything they wanted to eat all day. All the others were having eggs that morning.

"Cheeseburgers in the morning?" said Clem. "What next?"

"You just wish you could have one," Suzie told him.

"Me, too!" said Jeff.

Just then Suzie's father walked in. He was wheeling a big red bike. "Happy birthday!" he said.

"Ohhh," said Suzie. "I love it." It was the most beautiful bicycle she had ever seen. It didn't have one scrape on it.

"Here," said Jeff, handing her a big box. "From Clem and me."

Suzie took off the paper. It was

a light for the bike. "Thank you," she said. "Thank you very much."

Jeff smiled. Clem said, "Oh, that's OK, Suzie. Happy birthday!"

They were being so nice, Suzie thought. Maybe she should tell them the secret, after all.

Then her father said, "Well, Suzie, do you want to give it a try?"

"We have to see this," her brothers said, laughing.

Suzie smiled. "Yes," she said. "I do want to give it a try. But it has to be on the barn hill."

"The barn hill?" asked Jeff. "That's the hardest place on the farm. It's all bumps!"

"That's where I'm going to ride," said Suzie.

"We try to help her and she won't let us," said Jeff.

Suzie wheeled the new bicycle over to the barn hill. Everyone went with her. No one said a thing.

When they got there, Suzie fixed the pedal. Then she put the box up, next to the bike. When she got on top of the box, they all looked a little surprised. Suzie turned and looked at them standing there. She smiled. "See you later!" she called.

And she was off! She was riding down the hill! She thought about how they must all look, standing there. She laughed. She felt better than she had in all her life.

All Kinds of Families

What is a family? Does a family always live together?
How about pets? Are they part of a family?
Are all families alike?
Which family in this unit did you like best?
Why?

On a piece of paper, answer these questions about a family you like. Then draw a picture of the family.

1. Who are the members of this family?
2. Why is this a nice family?
3. What do you wish this family would do?

Jobs for All

Do you help in your house?

Think of the jobs people did in the stories you have read. Look back at the stories if you have to.

—Who cooked Suzie's dinner at night?
—What job at home did Jasmine have?
—What did Sia and her brothers and sisters do to help the family?

Look at the pictures below. Each person is helping in some way. Tell what each person is doing to help.

On a piece of paper, write the names of three jobs you would like to do to help around your house. Then tell a friend why you would like to do these jobs.

Busy Hands

The Orchard Toy Shop

by Carolyn Sherwin Bailey

In a building in Salem, Massachusetts, there is a room full of toys. Most of the toys are made of wood. There are wooden dolls, doll houses, and doll chairs, beds, and tables. There are puppets with arms and legs that move. There are wooden tops and blocks. There are drums and whistles. These toys belonged to children of early Americans.

Some of the wooden toys were made by a boy named Robert Manning. Robert was only 12 years old when he made the toys. The year was 1839.

Robert had an older brother named Richard. He also had an older sister named Rebecca.

Robert's father grew fruit trees. He grew all the trees from seeds.

The seeds had come from England on a boat. Mr. Manning took great care in growing the trees. No one else in Salem, Massachusetts, had fruit trees as fine as his. The fruits he grew were new to the United States.

Robert could smell the fruit trees as he worked. He could smell pears, apples, peaches, and cherries.

Robert was making a doll. He was making a table and doll dishes, too. He was making a doll bed that rocked. He liked using tools. He liked using old fruit wood for the toys. His shop was the fruit-packing house.

Many years before, in 1679, the first Mannings came to America. They came on a ship. In Massachusetts, they built their first home.

Captain Nicholas Manning brought tools for building from England. He was not a builder, but he loved to build. He loved to make beautiful things for the house.

Robert had tools like those of Captain Nicholas Manning. He had a square to help him cut the wood evenly. He had a brace and bit to make holes. He had sandpaper to make the wood smooth. The tools were very much like tools we have today. Have you seen tools like these?

Robert loved the old house Captain Manning had built. He loved the way the rooms looked. He made toys that looked like things in the old house. Captain Manning and other Mannings after him had made the tables and chairs and other things in the old house.

With apple wood, Robert made a small table. It was large enough for a small set of dishes.

Robert had made a set of dishes from cherry wood. It took a whole winter to make them. There were six plates, six cups, two cake dishes, two candlesticks, a cup for cream, and a little bowl.

Robert's brother, Richard, painted fruit on the dishes. The fruit looked real.

This day, Robert was just finishing the table. Richard came into the packing house.

"Where is the doll's bed?" he asked. "I would like to paint it today. Rebecca has made a pillow and a cover for it."

Robert took the bed from its hiding place. It was also of fruit wood. It had a rounded top and high sides. The legs were made to rock.

"It looks just like the bed in the old house," said Richard.

"Look at this," said Robert. He showed Richard a toy fireplace made from apple wood.

"It looks just like the fireplace in Captain Manning's house, too."

"I like that old house," said Robert. "It makes me think of new ways to make toys."

Robert was almost finished with the table. He took a small wooden doll from a box. She was just big enough to eat from the dishes. He put her near the table.

Rebecca had made her a blue and white dress. She had a hat made of straw. Her arms and legs could move.

Robert made all these toys for a friend. She was a girl named Isabel. Just as Robert put down the doll, Isabel came to the door.

"Oh, how nice!" she said. She touched the table. It was almost finished.

Richard laughed. "Ah, ha," he said. "Now we know who will get all these toys. We wondered why he was making them."

"Are they for me?" asked Isabel. "And the doll, too?"

"Yes, you may have them all," said Robert. "With all these things, you can have a room just like our great-great-grandfather and grandmother."

Isabel took them all home that very day.

When Robert was 15, he took over his father's fruit trees. He cared for them as well as his father had. Everyone knew about his fruits. He wrote for a newspaper. He wrote about care of fruit trees and gardens. Seeds from his trees started trees all over the United States.

Some of the fruit trees Robert Manning planted still live.

The toys he made for his friend Isabel can still be seen in Salem, Massachusetts. They are only toys, but they show how the early Americans lived.

Busy Carpenters

The song of the saw
Is true
As we cut the boards
In two.

The song of the plane
Is sweet
As the shavings curl
At our feet.

And the song of the hammer
Is good
As we drive the nails
In the wood.

—James S. Tippett

Take This Hammer

by Sam and Beryl Epstein

Can you drive a nail into a board with this hammer?

Try it.

Hit the nail with the flat end of the hammer head. The steel head is hard and heavy.

Bang! Bang! Bang! Each blow drives the nail deeper into the wood.

What other things could you use to drive a nail into a board?

Could you hammer a nail with a bar of soap?

Try it.

When you hit the nail with the soap do you drive the nail into the soap?

Soap is too soft for driving nails. You need something hard.

The hammer did the job because its steel head is hard.

Could you use a ruler to drive a nail? Try it.

Does the ruler drive the nail into the board? Or does the nail stay just where it is?

The ruler is too light for driving nails. You need something heavy.

The hammer did the job because its steel head is heavy.

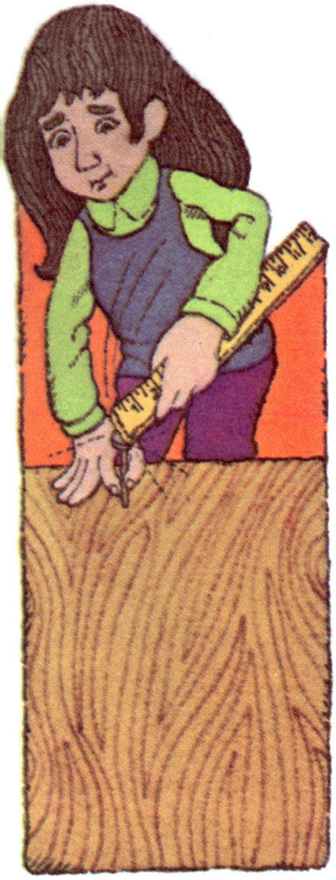

A carpenter uses a hammer like this to build a house. Every day the carpenter drives nails with a hammer.

If the carpenter drives a nail in the wrong place, how can it be pulled out?

Try pulling a nail out of a board with your fingers. Why won't the nail come out?

Try the other end of the hammer head. It is called a claw. The hard, strong steel claw grabs the nail and pulls it out.

Some hammers are very big. A sledge hammer is so big that only someone very strong can pick it up.

Did you ever see a small hammer?

This man is fixing a watch. He is using a tiny hammer.

Most hammers are hard and heavy.

Can you think of a hammer that is light and soft?

What kind of hammer does a drummer use to bang a drum?

Would a heavy hammer break the drum?

A drummer uses a light hammer with a head made of soft cloth.

Do all hammers have handles?

Could you use a stone for a hammer?

Try it. Find a stone that fits into your hand. Try to drive a nail with it.

If the stone is not very hard, it may break.

If the stone is hard enough, it will be a good hammer. It can be your hammer stone.

Does your hammer stone have a handle? Does your arm act like the handle of your hammer stone?

A hammer stone was the first tool that people used. They used it to break open nuts. They used it to knock off edges on other stones. In that way, they could make a stone knife and an arrow head.

Are these workers using a hammer to knock down this brick wall?

Is that big ball a kind of hammer? When it hits the wall, does it move something?

Crash! Crash! Crash! Every time the ball hits, it sends bricks flying through the air.

Are these workers using a hammer to drive that big pole into the ground?

Is this a kind of hammer?

Yes, it is a very big hammer called a pile driver.

Most hammers are used for building things or for doing other kinds of work.

Can you think of a way to play a game with hammers?

These children are playing with wooden hammers. They are using the hammers to drive wooden balls across the grass.

The hammers they are playing with are called mallets. Their game is called croquet.

Can you think of any other games to play with hammers?

Is a baseball bat a kind of hammer?

Can you think of a way to play music with hammers?

This woman is playing music on a xylophone. She uses little hammers to hit the wooden bars and make them move quickly. Each bar sounds a different note.

Look inside a piano. Do you see all the small felt hammers?

Hit one of the keys of the piano. Does one of the little hammers hit a wire? Does the wire make a sound?

Can you play music by hitting piano keys and making the little hammers sound one note after another?

How does a doctor use this hammer? To tap your knees. If your leg doesn't go up in the air, it shows that something is wrong.

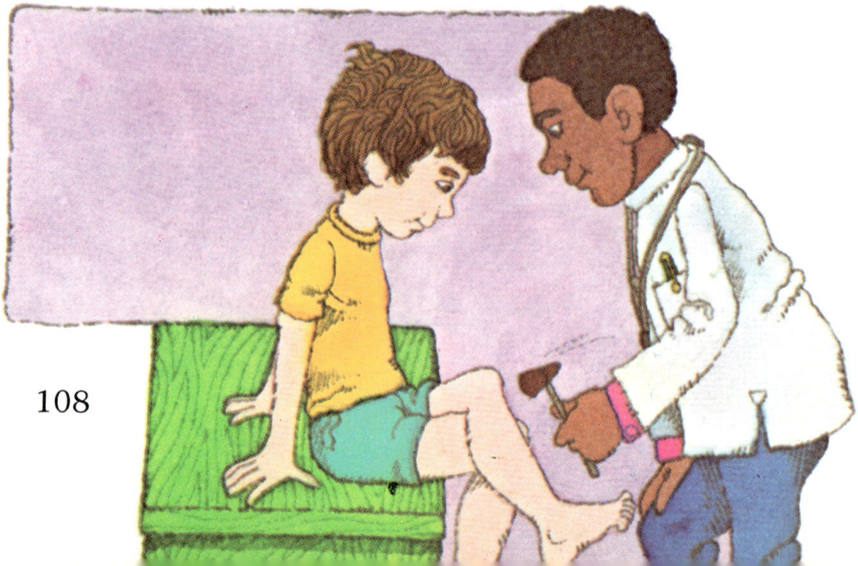

How does a judge use this hammer? To bang it down and say, "Order! Order!" A judge's hammer is called a gavel.

Do you know about other people who use special kinds of hammers?

How many different kinds of hammers can you think of?

Pancakes, Pancakes!

by Eric Carle

"Cock-a-doodle-doo!" went the rooster.

Jack woke up and looked out of the window. The sun was coming up.

"How hungry I am. I could eat a large pancake for breakfast," said Jack.

Jack's mother was already busy. Jack sat down at the kitchen table.

"Mother," he asked, "may I have a large pancake for breakfast?"

"I have a lot of work to do," she answered. "If you want a pancake, you will have to help me."

"What should I do?" asked Jack.

"First we will need flour to make a pancake," she said.

"Go out to the wheat field. Cut as much wheat as your donkey can carry. Then take the wheat

to the mill. The miller will make
the wheat into flour."

Jack rode his donkey
to the wheat field. When he had cut
enough wheat, he put it
on his donkey's back. He led the donkey
to the mill.

"Can you make this wheat into flour
for me?" Jack asked the miller.
"I need it to make a large pancake."

"First, we'll have to get the grain out of its covering," said the miller.

He handed Jack a stick with a shorter stick held onto it. The miller put the wheat on the ground. He took another stick. He began to beat the wheat. Jack helped him. Soon there was a small pile of grain.

The miller took the grain into the mill house. He put the grain on a large flat stone. On top

of that stone was a round mill stone. The mill stone was turned by a water wheel outside. The mill stone turned round and round. It ground the wheat—first into small bits, then into flour.

At last, the miller handed Jack a bag of flour. Then he smiled and said, "Here's a handful of grain. You may need it."

Jack did not know what the grain was for. He put it in his pocket. He rode home with the bag of flour under his arm.

"Here is the flour," said Jack. "Now let's make the pancake! I'm hungry!"

"But we need an egg," his mother said. "See if the black hen has one."

Jack went to the hen house. The black hen said, "Cluck, cluck." But she had no eggs.

"Ah," said Jack, "You are hungry. So am I!" Jack reached into his pocket.

He took out the grain. He gave it to the hen.

The black hen went to her nest. There she sat, very still, for a long time. Jack waited and waited.

He was ready to give up. Just then, the hen said, "Cluck, cluck" again. There was an egg.

Carefully, Jack took the egg from the nest. He ran back to the house.

"Here is an egg, Mother. Let's make a pancake. I'm so hungry!" said Jack.

His mother said, "Now we need some milk. Go to the field. See if the spotted cow has milk for you."

She handed him a pail and a stool.

In the field, Jack put his stool next to the cow. He put a leg on each side of the pail. He started milking. The milk went into the pail. When he had enough, he patted the cow on her nose. He took the milk back to the house.

"Here's the milk. Can you make the pancake now?" said Jack.

"No, not yet. We need some butter," said his mother. She went to the store room next to the kitchen. She came back with the butter churn. She took the cream off the top of the milk. She put the cream into the butter churn.

Now it was Jack's turn to work again. He began to pull and push

the churn handle. Up and down, up and down went the handle. The cream got thicker. The handle seemed to get heavier. And then the cream turned to golden butter.

"I am so hungry!" said Jack. "Let's make the pancake."

But his mother said, "Go to the wood pile and bring me some logs. And some small bits of wood. I need wood to build up the fire."

Jack brought the fire wood.

"Now?" he asked.

But his mother said, "Wouldn't you like something sweet to go with your pancake? Go downstairs and look for something sweet."

She gave Jack a candle. He went downstairs.

There were apple jelly, maple syrup, honey, peach jam, and strawberry jam. He took the strawberry jam.

He carried it back upstairs to his mother.

In the kitchen, Jack's mother started the fire. On the table she put the flour, the egg, the milk, and the butter. She made room for a mixing bowl and a cup, a large wooden spoon, and a frying pan. She also put out a plate, a knife, a fork, and a spoon. Jack made room for the strawberry jam.

"Put a cup of flour in the bowl," said his mother.

"Break an egg into the flour and mix it."

"Pour a cup of milk over the flour and egg. Now mix it again."

At last the batter was smooth, without any lumps.

Jack's mother put the frying pan over the fire. She put a bit of butter in the pan. The butter melted fast. She said to Jack, "Now pour some batter into the hot pan."

After a minute or two, she looked at the underside of the pancake. It was golden brown.

"Now watch," she said. "I'll turn the pancake over. Ready?"

"Ready!" shouted Jack.

"Flip," said his mother. Up and over went the pancake high in the air.

"Watch out!" yelled Jack.

But his mother caught the pancake right in the middle of the pan.

In a few more minutes, the pancake was brown on the other side.

"Bring me your plate," said his mother. She put the pancake on Jack's plate.

"Shall I put strawberry jam on it?" she asked.

"Yummmm," was all Jack could say.

"And now, Jack," his mother started to say.

Jack said, "Oh, Mama, I know what to do now!"

Recipe for Strawberry Jam

Here is an easy way to make strawberry jam. It is very good with bread or with Pancakes a la Jack.

What you need to make the jam:

- 5 cups fresh strawberries
- 5 cups sugar
- 5 tablespoons lemon juice

Tools you need:

- 1 large pot
- 1 large spoon
- 1 measuring cup
- 1 tablespoon
- 1 deep steel pan

This is what to do:

1. Wash the strawberries and take off the hulls.
2. In the pot, put a layer of strawberries. Then add a layer of sugar. Do this again until all the strawberries and sugar are in the pot.
3. Heat the pot until juice begins to come to the top.
4. Skim the foam from the top with the spoon.
5. Boil for 7 minutes.
6. Now add the lemon juice.
7. Boil for 3 more minutes.
8. Take from the heat.
9. Put in the large steel pan.
10. Let the jam stand overnight.

In the morning, do you know what to do? Right! Put it on your pancakes or bread and eat!

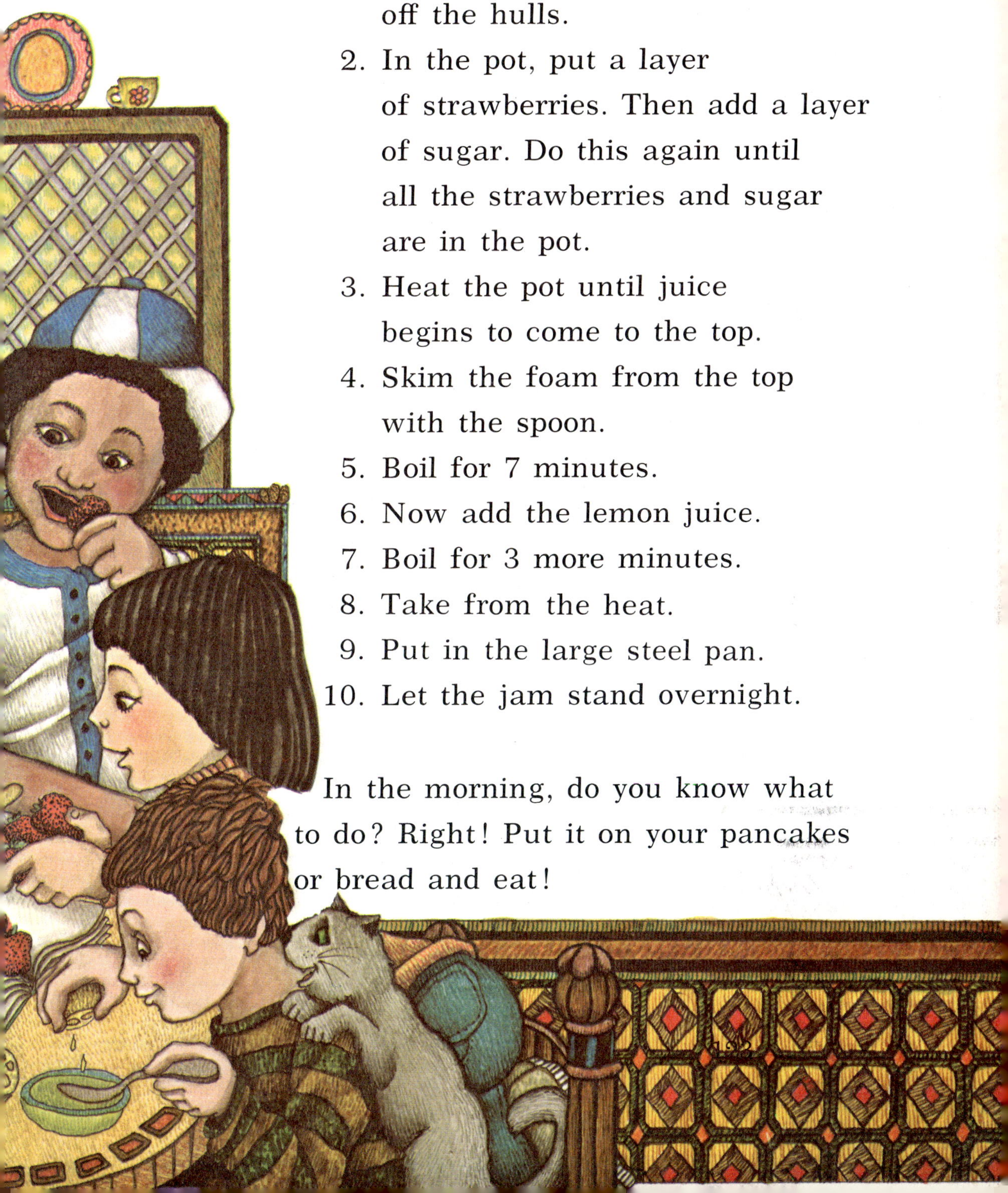

Busy Wheels

by Peter Lippman

In the city, wheels are turning everywhere.

Early in the morning, garbage trucks roll down the street. Cans bang. People call to one another.

Trucks with brushes on wheels clean the streets and pick up the dirt.

People ride to work in buses. People wheel their babies on the sidewalks.

Everyone is on the move!

Busy wheels help them move faster.

When a fire breaks out, the fire trucks come as fast as they can. Whistles blow. Cars get out of the way of fire trucks.

In the afternoon, wheels bring children home from school. Some children ride school buses. Some ride on bicycles. Others go by car.

After school, an ice cream cone tastes good. A truck can bring ice cream right to your street.

Mail moves on wheels, too. And so do animals. Wherever you look, something is rolling along.

Busy wheels help to build roads. Bulldozers and diesel shovels dig up the dirt. Dump trucks move it out of the way. Big heavy rollers make the road smooth.

In the country, other kinds of wheels are at work. Tractors pull plows and wagons. Reapers cut the crops. Trucks carry the cows' milk from the farm to the city.

Busy wheels never stop! In winter, snow plows push the snow out of the road. Snow blowers make the snow fly into the air and out of the way. Wheels make the road safe for other wheels.

Some people live on wheels. They drive their trailers and campers from place to place. Sometimes they stop just for the night.

Sometimes they stay in the same place for a long time. Trailers have kitchens and beds and even bathrooms. A home on wheels is fun.

Some people like to move fast! Their racing cars zoom around and around the track. People cheer. Who will be the lucky winner?

Sometimes wheels go too fast. Then there is a crash. Tow trucks take away the crashed cars. Ambulances take the people who have been hurt to the hospital.

At the end of the day, train wheels bring fathers and mothers back from the city. Car wheels are waiting to take them home.

There are even wheels to carry wheels. Every day, trains carry new cars to all parts of the country. The cars are taken off the train, and then they are ready to ride on their own wheels.

Some people go places in airplanes. Planes fly in the air. On the ground, they roll on wheels. Trucks carrying gas for the plane roll around the air field. Trucks with bags and trucks with food roll around the air field. Wheels are very busy at the airports!

Wheels have even gone to the moon. The astronauts ride on wheels through the moon dust.

Everywhere you look, busy wheels are turning!

Tools, Tools Everywhere

Pretend you are in the woods. You are a long way from a store or other people. You want to put up your tent, but you forgot to bring a hammer.

How would you make your own hammer? That's right! You would have to use the things you find in the woods.

On a piece of paper, draw pictures of all the different kinds of hammers you could make by using things you find in the woods. Then look at a friend's pictures. Which hammer would probably work best? Why?

Wheels Are Busy

Here is a picture of a wheel.

On a piece of paper, write as many things as you can that the wheel could be used for. These pictures show two uses for the wheel. Try to write many more.

Look at the pictures below. All of these things have wheels. What job does each thing do?

Now think of how people could do these jobs without wheels to help them. Draw pictures that show how people could do each job without wheels.

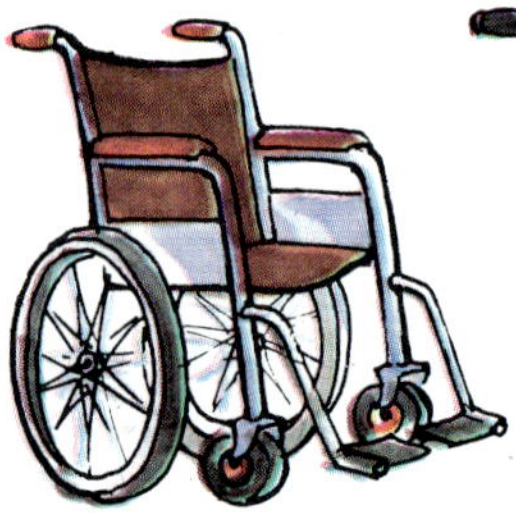

Come See the Sea

Astronauts and Aquanauts

Astronauts
aquanauts
dare to explore
places that no one has been to before.

People exploring
above
or below
need houses to live in
wherever they go.

—Joanne Oppenheim

Jacques Cousteau: Underwater Pioneer

by Charles N. Heckelmann

What do you think of when you hear the word "pioneer"? Do you think of people in covered wagons and log houses? Those pioneers are an important part of our country's past. But there are pioneers today, too.

Just what is a pioneer? A pioneer is someone who does something before anyone else does it. The first person to climb a mountain is a pioneer. The first person to go to the moon is a pioneer. The first person to do some special kind of work is a pioneer.

This story is about a pioneer of the undersea world. His name is Jacques Cousteau.

Jacques was born in France in 1910. When he was young, Jacques and his family went to many places.

When he grew up, Jacques went into the navy. While he was in the navy, he learned to love the sea and all its interesting fishes and plants.

When he left the navy, Jacques bought his own ship. He used that ship for many years to explore the oceans.

Jacques Cousteau has done more than any other person to open up the undersea world. The sea is full of important things. Fish and plant foods are found in its waters. These foods are very important to the men, women, and children who live on Earth.

You may have seen Jacques Cousteau on television. You probably know that he does most of his work under water. But do you know that he made many of the things he uses under water? The Aqua-lung is one people know best. This is another way that Cousteau is a pioneer.

The Aqua-lung lets divers breathe under water. It has its own air.

With it, a diver can stay under water for a long time. The diver can go as deep as 65 meters and still get enough air to breathe.

Cousteau was one of the first people to take pictures under water. He made a very special camera. It is very heavy out of the water. But under water, it is so light that it floats! With this camera, Cousteau can take pictures of all kinds of fish. He can also take pictures of sunken ships, rocks, and other things on the sea floor.

Cousteau made many other things to use under water. The diving saucer is one of the most important things Cousteau made.

The diving saucer is like a tiny space ship. It is called a saucer because of the way it looks. It looks like two saucers, one upside down on top of the other.

Two people can ride in the saucer.

They can make it go up or down. They can also make it stand still. The saucer has headlights that shine through the deep water.

The saucer can drop 300 meters in 20 minutes. Inside the saucer, the air stays fresh and clean.

Cameras on the saucer take pictures of all the things that swim about in the underwater world. There are fish, sea worms, sharks, and many kinds of sea flowers. There are also sea animals that look like flowers.

The people in the saucer can hear sea noises. Special telephones let them do this.

Other telephones on Cousteau's ship are used to talk to the saucer. As it moves through the water, the saucer gives off a sound. No matter where the saucer goes, the ship can keep track of it.

The saucer has a big arm with a claw on it. The claw can catch fish. It can also pick up things from the sea floor.

With the saucer and the Aqua-lung, Cousteau has explored the seas all over the world. He has seen fish no one had ever seen before. He has found mountains and gardens under the sea. He has swum with sea turtles and sea lions. He has watched sharks, and he has heard whales talk.

He has also found sunken ships.

Many of these ships sank many, many years before. One ship has been at the bottom of the sea for more than 2,000 years.

Cousteau has made movies about the sea. He has written books. But most people know of him through his television shows. Through television, Cousteau has reached people all over the world. He has opened up the undersea world to them.

Cousteau has also been working to keep our oceans clean. He works with people all over the world. Together they try to teach people how important it is to take care of the seas.

This means we must keep our rivers clean, too. Pollution in our rivers soon goes into the oceans. The animals, fish, and plant foods of the oceans are killed by this pollution. These foods are needed to feed people all over the world.

Cousteau says, "We must take better care of our oceans."

Will you help?

A Whale

I know a funny thing about
A whale who has a water spout.
He swallows too much ocean in
And needs to blow some out.

—Myra Cohn Livingston

The Dragon Island

by Florence Holbrook

Once there was a goddess of the sea who loved the people of Japan. Often she came out of the water at sunset. Then she would sit on a high rock near the water and tell stories to the children.

She would tell wonderful stories about the strange fishes under the sea. She told about fair maidens that live deep down in the sea.

"Are there no children in the sea? Why don't they come out to play with us?" the children asked.

"Sometime they will come. You must keep on wishing for them," answered the goddess.

Then the goddess would sing to the children. Her voice was so sweet that the evening star would stand still and listen to her song.

"Please show us how the water rises and falls," the children said.

Then the goddess would hold up a magic stone and say, "Water, rise!" The waves would come in faster and faster all about the rock.

When the goddess put down the stone and said, "Water, fall," the waves would be still. The water would roll back quickly to the deep sea.

She was goddess of the storm as well as of the sea. Sometimes the children would say, "Goddess, please make us a storm."

She never said no to what they asked. So the rain fell and the thunder rolled. The rain would fall all about them. But the goddess did not let it fall on them. They were never afraid of the lightning. They knew the goddess would not let it touch them.

One of the goddess's sea animals was a dragon. It often played in the water near the shore.

The children never thought of being afraid. The sea animals belonged to their friend.

One day, the dragon picked up a little child in its mouth. Soon, it had eaten the child. Everyone was very sad and angry.

"O goddess," the people cried, "come to us! The dragon has taken a child!"

The goddess was angry with the dragon.

"Dragon, come to me!" she called.

The dragon was frightened, but it came right away. It had to do what the goddess said.

"You will never again play in the water with the other sea animals. You will be a rocky island. There will be trees and plants on you. After a time, people will not remember that you were once a dragon."

The dragon found that it could no longer move. It was changing into rock. Trees and plants grew on its back. It WAS an island.

People looked at the island and said, "That was once the dragon."

The children of the sea maidens and the children of the people played together on the island. They had many happy times.

In Japan there are many pictures of the goddess. In the pictures, the goddess is changing the dragon into an island.

When children are told the story, they always wonder, "Where is the island now?"

Just as the goddess said, no one remembers which island was the dragon.

No one remembers, but sometimes small islands look like dragons and monsters to people looking out on the sea.

The Monster of Loch Ness

by Martha Shogren

Loch Ness is a beautiful lake in Scotland. It is also a very special lake. Loch Ness is special because many people think there is a sea monster in it. But no one knows what the monster is. No one knows how big it is. And some people don't think it is there at all!

Why do many people think a monster is in the lake? They say they have seen it there. People riding by the lake in cars, buses, or trains have seen something in the water. They say it looked like a monster. Other people sitting by the lake have seen something, too. They say that it was the monster.

What does the monster look like? Some people say it is about nine meters long. They say it has a large body with a small head on top of a long neck. They say that it swims with its head high out of the water. It moves very fast through the lake.

Scientists have found that Loch Ness could be a good place for a sea monster to live. It is very big, and it is very deep. It also has many fish that a monster could eat.

If there is a monster in Loch Ness, how did it get there? No one is sure.

Loch Ness does run into the sea.
But the opening is too small
for a large sea monster to get through.

This makes some scientists think
that at one time the opening was larger.
Sea monsters may have come
into the lake. Then an earthquake may
have blocked the opening to the sea.
The sea monsters could not get
out of the lake.

Some scientists think the monster is a very, very old kind of animal. They think it may be a kind of animal that lived in the days of the dinosaurs. They say that it may be a sea animal called plesiosaur (PLEES-ee-o-sawr) which lived in those days.

Plesiosaur had a long, thin neck and a very small head. It had flippers and a short, fat tail. Scientists think it swam with its head high out of the water.

Does this sound like the Loch Ness monster? Do you think the scientists may be right?

For many years people have tried to learn more about the monster. Many people have taken pictures. A special kind of picture was taken by an echo sounder on a fishing boat. It shows something large under the water.

An echo sounder is something like radar. It can tell what is under the water. It can tell if fish are nearby. It can tell if rocks are close to the boat.

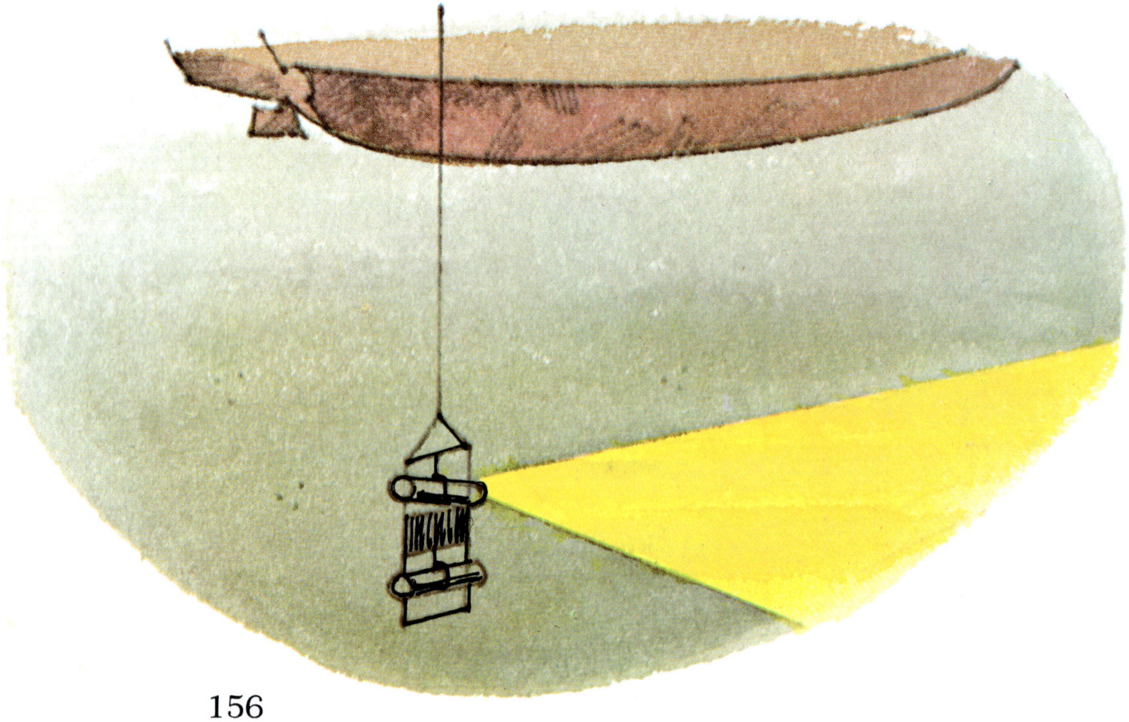

One day a fishing boat was out looking for fish. The echo sounder was turned on. It showed something very big under the boat. The people on the boat could not believe their eyes. It must be the monster!

Cameras have also taken pictures of something in Loch Ness. One picture shows three dark humps. The man who took the picture said he saw a small head on a long neck, too. But the monster moved its head before the man could take the picture.

Pictures taken by other people do show the head and the long neck.

In May, 1960, a man was visiting Loch Ness. He saw something move in the water. Was it the monster? He walked out into the water with his camera. His picture shows an animal with a large black body and a long neck. It does look something like a plesiosaur.

Many, many people say they have seen the monster. They have even given it a name. They call it "Nessie."

Some people say they have seen Nessie more than once. Often more than one person sees it at the same time. Maybe some of the people who say they have seen Nessie are joking. But they can't all be joking!

Every summer, people come to Loch Ness. They all hope to see Nessie. Sometimes tricks are played on them. Once someone tied some barrels together and put a metal animal head on the front. The "barrel monster" was pulled across the lake. People thought they were seeing Nessie.

Another time, large footprints were found along the shore. People thought they were made by Nessie. But it was a joke. Someone had made the prints with a hippopotamus foot!

People laughed at the tricks. They knew these tricks were not really the monster. Still no one knows what the monster really is.

But the people in Scotland say, "There is something out there." Now many scientists say this, too.

What do you think it is?

The Bottom of the Sea

Let's Go Down!

. . . to the bottom of the sea.
What do you see?
What if you went deeper
than anyone else?
What strange sea animals
might you see?

Draw a picture of the bottom of the sea and a strange sea animal. Give your sea animal a strange sea name. Tell what the animal does. Tell about your animal by using some words that sound like the sea or water.

Going New Places

Some pioneers explore the bottom of the sea. Some explore outer space. Pretend you are going into outer space. On a piece of paper, write a story about your trip.

Here is one way to start your story.

Jacques Cousteau and I were exploring the bottom of the sea. Suddenly the diving saucer started to rise. Up, up it went out of the sea and into space. It went higher and higher until . . . .

Finding My Place

Infinity

Big Sky Ranch
R.F.D. #3
Kalispell,
Montana,
59901,
U.S.A.,
North America,
Western Hemisphere,
The World,
Space,
Solar System,
Our Galaxy,
The Universe.

Star bright,
Space light,
First star I see tonight,
I wish I may,
I wish I might,
Have the wish
I wish tonight.

Just think . . .
The world is like a space ship.
It turns in space
And we ride on it.
All people ride together
On Space Ship Earth.

—Betty Miles and Joan Blos

The Dancing Class

by Shelley List

Angela's mother read about the dancing classes in the newspaper. It said boys and girls could take dance lessons at the Community Center.

Angela said, "Momma, please let me take dancing lessons. Please!"

Angela was seven years old. She had wanted to take dancing lessons ever since she saw some dancers on TV. The women all wore beautiful white dresses, and they moved like water. Angela wanted to dance just like them.

So one snowy Saturday morning, Angela and her mother rode the bus downtown to the Community Center. When she saw the building, Angela thought they had come to the wrong place. It looked like a store, not a dancing school!

"It's called a store front," said Angela's mother. "It used to be a cleaners. They have all kinds of classes here. You can learn to sing, or paint, or act. And you can learn to dance!"

When they went inside, Angela hid behind her mother. She was a little afraid now that she was here. She looked out from behind her mother's coat at the teacher.

"Hello. I'm Sandy," the teacher said with a big smile. "I know how you feel. I took dancing lessons too, when I was as old as you are."

Angela felt better then, so she took off her coat.

Sandy was a tall young woman. She seemed nice. Angela could not wait

to see her dance. She stood so straight and walked so beautifully.

Angela wore the black tights her mother had bought her. They made her feel like a real dancer!

Sandy took Angela and her mother into a large room. Some children were sitting on the floor, waiting for class to begin.

In a room in the back, some girls and boys were practicing a play. Angela saw her friend Charleen. She came to the Center two times a week. Charleen loved plays.

But for Angela, dancing was everything! She wanted to be a dancer.

"At first," said Sandy, "you will not do much dancing, only exercises. But soon you will be dancing in the yearly show."

Angela's mother left to do some shopping. Down went Angela's head. She bit her lip and looked down at her feet.

Al, a boy in the class, came over to her.

"My name is Al. What's your name?" he asked.

"Angela," she said very softly.

"Listen," Al said, "don't be afraid. When I first came to the Center, I was all by myself. I didn't know anybody. And everyone was bigger than me. But now I have lots of friends. And you will, too."

Sandy was ready to begin the class.

"OK, everybody, take your places."

There were nine children. Al stood next to Angela so she wouldn't feel so alone.

"Lie down on your sides," Sandy said. "Now move your legs back and forth, back and forth."

Then Sandy said, "Everybody up! Let's straighten out the rows. Now everyone get down on your knees. I have a surprise for you."

Angela got quickly on her knees.

A tall young man came into the room. He began to play a drum. The children moved from side to side. Angela liked the sound. The beat of the drum made it easier to do the exercise.

"All right, everybody. Up on your feet. Let's do some of the dance positions," said Sandy.

Sandy placed her feet so they made a *V*.

"This is called first position," she said. "Now, bend your knees out, and keep your feet on the ground. This is called a plié (plee-AY)."

It was hard for Angela to bend her knees without lifting the backs of her feet, but she did it.

"That's pretty good for the first time," said Al.

"OK, everybody," Sandy said, "let's leap across the floor to end the class."

Everyone lined up in one corner. Angela went to the end of the line

because she didn't know how to leap. The bigger children in front showed her how. They just ran slowly with their legs stretched way out in front and back. Angela tried, and it felt good.

"Good, Angela, that's very good for the first time," Sandy said.

At the end of the class, Angela's mother came to pick her up. Angela couldn't stop smiling. She couldn't wait until next Saturday.

Enuk, My Son

by Claire Fejes

When the sun comes out
And winter darkness ends,
When hundreds of ducks and geese
Honk overhead as they fly north,
The Eskimos of Tigara know it
is time
To hunt the great whale.

Enuk heard his dog growl and ran out of his sod house. The ducks were overhead! During the time of the long nights, he had eaten fish and bear meat.

How good duck soup would taste now! He could hardly wait for the whale feast. Muktuk, the outer skin of the whale, was Enuk's favorite food.

The village was getting ready for the whale hunt. Enuk's father was an umelik, a captain of the whalers. On his mukluks was the white band of the whale hunter. Mukluks are the fur boots Eskimos wear. His pants were made of bear skin.

The men fixed the broken parts of the whaling boat. The women put the walrus skins together with small, even stitches. Then the men stretched the skins over the wooden frame of the boat.

Early the next morning, the north wind blew. The whales were going north along the shores of Tigara. They came up in open water to spout high up in the air.

Father packed the tent, clothes, and food on the sled. Enuk helped his mother hook the dog team to the sled. Baby sat on Mother's back, covered with furs. Then Father shouted, "Go!"

Suddenly they were off! The dog team stopped near the open water. It was

several miles from the village. They took the things from the sled and put up the tent. They fixed the dogs so they could not run off. Then they made camp on the ice.

The hunters waited, sitting on the sleds. Their skin boat was waiting at the edge of the sea. The harpoon was ready in the boat.

Enuk kept a fire going in the tent. He carried pails of clean snow to melt. His mother pulled the feathers from a duck, cut it, and put it in the pot to cook. Then she fed the baby.

Enuk carried hot duck soup to his father and the men. He brought plates and spoons and bread that his mother had baked.

After he ate, he threw fish to the hungry dogs.

In the cold, silent morning, the hunters waited, sleeping on the ice. The captain kept watch.

After the Whale

Early the next morning, Enuk brought hot tea.

"Stay with us, we need you in the boat," said his father.

He gave Enuk a small whale made of ivory.

"Here is a lucky charm for you, Enuk. My father gave it to me when I first went whaling. It belonged to his great-great-grandfather."

The red sun sank, and icy wind burned Enuk's face. He waited with the hunters. The waiting made him sleepy. He fell asleep. Someone poked him sharply in the ribs.

When he opened his eyes, the men were already in the skin boat. Enuk jumped in and grabbed a paddle.

"The whale has tiny eyes, but sharp ears," his father said. "Don't make a sound when you see him."

Suddenly, they saw a spouting.

Then a flash of a tail. Quickly, quickly the whale came closer.

Enuk opened his mouth in fear. He was so frightened that he paddled backward!

His father shot the harpoon. The whale dived, splashing the men with water. The harpoon fell off the whale's back. He swam away under the ice pack.

That night there was much joking about the "boy who paddled backward."

His father put his arm around Enuk. He said, "Never mind, my son. Next time you will go straight ahead."

Days and nights the men waited for the whale to come again.

The sun turned the snow pink. Ice broke off and went into the sea with a splishhhhhh.

Enuk shot a duck while they waited. The men hunted white whales called beluga.

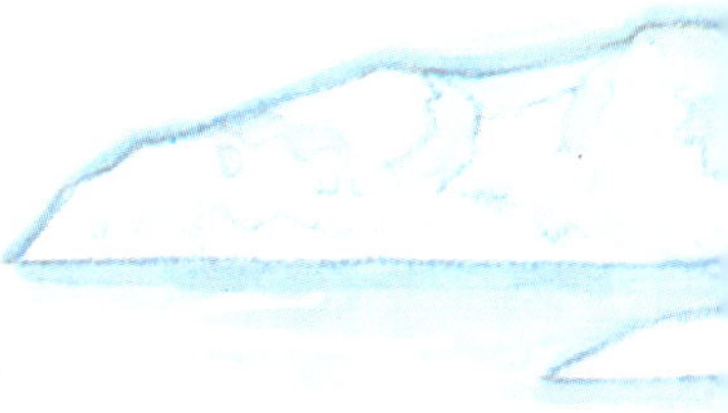

The sun cracked the ice around them. If the ice broke off, they might float out to sea.

On the 14th day, they heard a puffing sound. A whale was blowing. They went after him!

This time Enuk paddled straight ahead. But he was still afraid.

His father's harpoon hit the whale. The whale dived under the water, dragging the line with him.

The boats closed in. The whale struggled. The water was red with whale blood. He was dead.

The hunters sang the whale-hunting song. They towed the whale to shore.

Everyone helped to pull the whale onto the ice. They began to cut up the whale.

Enuk went back to the village by dog team.

"The whale is dead," he shouted. "The great whale is dead."

Bells rang. The children ran from the school house. Even the teacher came running. Now there would be food for all.

When the sun melts the snow
in the village,
When the sea gulls arrive
by the hundreds,
To eat the fish in the sea,
When the murres nest
on the rocky cliffs
And the wild flowers burst up
from the tundra,
The Eskimos of Tigara know
It is time for Nalukatuk,
the whaling feast.

On the first day of the feast, Enuk's mother boiled whale meat. She fried doughnuts in whale oil.

Enuk ate so much muktuk, he could hardly move.

On the second day of the feast, Enuk was tossed up high in the air. He was tossed from a large walrus hide held by the others.

On the next day of the feast, Enuk's mother surprised him. She put a new pair of mukluks under his bed. They had a white band on top like his father's.

"You have worked in the whaling boat," she said. "You are a man now, Enuk, my son."

That evening was the Nalukatuk Dance. The drummers beat loudly, "Aie, aie, aie, aie."

Enuk stomped his new mukluks in time. Around his neck swung his lucky ivory whale.

On the last day of the feast,
Enuk stood with his mother and father.
He gave away slices of whale fin,
as his great-great-grandfather
had done before him.

He would always remember his first
whale hunt.

A Pet for Rosita

by Linda Hirschmann

"Come on, Rosita, come play stickball," Tony called. He swung his stick and waited for the pitch.

"No," said Rosita, with her head down. She wasn't used to city games yet. Ball games should be played in parks. With real bats. How could she play ball with all the buildings in the way?

"The more players, the more fun," Amy said.

Rosita shook her head and stepped back. What if she missed the ball or fell over the curb? She didn't want Tony or Amy to laugh at her.

"Come on," Amy said and threw the ball at her.

Rosita wasn't ready. The ball flew past her and landed in a litter basket.

"Basket," Amy yelled. "Two points." She and Tony laughed. Rosita was sure they were laughing at her. She turned and ran into her apartment house.

In her apartment, her older brother Carlos was helping their mother. They talked happily as they worked.

"Hello," said Carlos. "We were just talking about you and your birthday present."

"Oh, is it a kitten?" Rosita asked. "Just like the one I used to have in Mexico?"

Her mother shook her head.

"You know the landlord's rule," Mrs. Perez said. "No animals."

"But a kitten's such a little animal," Rosita said.

"The landlord thinks all animals are the same," said Carlos. "He'd say the same thing about a kitten that he'd say about an elephant. No animals!"

Rosita said nothing. What was the use? Cities mean no pets and ball games in the street.

She looked out the window. Amy was at bat.

"Try to guess what your birthday present is," said Carlos. "I know you can't, no matter what you guess."

Rosita didn't even try. She watched the stickball game. It looked like fun.

Rosita woke early on her birthday. Before she opened her eyes, she wished —hard—for a furry white kitten.

"Get up, Birthday Girl," Mrs. Perez called and pulled back the sheet.

Rosita jumped out of bed.
The first thing she saw was her cake.

"Oh, Mama, how beautiful!"
Her cake, icy white, was covered with tiny roses.

"*Rositas* for Rosita." Her mother kissed her.

"And more roses for Rosita," Carlos said. He gave her a tiny rose bush.

"A *rosita* plant that will grow near the window," he said.

"It's not a kitten," Mrs. Perez said, "but it is like a pet. You have to take care of it, and you should talk to it, too. Plants grow best when people talk to them."

"Plants can't talk back," thought Rosita, "or play." But she didn't say that out loud. Instead, she kissed her mother and Carlos and thanked them for the present.

After breakfast, Mrs. Perez went to work. Then Carlos sent Rosita to the store.

"Get some eggs and some bread," he said.

The street was noisy and there were many people. Music floated from windows. Children played games and talked. People sat on front steps and talked. People stuck their heads out of their windows and talked with friends in the apartments above. They called to their children in the street below. Everyone on the street talked. Everyone but Rosita.

Rosita had nothing to talk about. She walked with her head down and thought about kittens all the way to the grocery store. She thought so hard about kittens she could almost hear one. She stopped.

She really did hear a kitten. Its meow came from the street next to the grocery store. Rosita looked in. Broken boxes were piled and tossed everywhere.

"Meow!" The sound came from a wooden box.

"You squeezed in, didn't you?" Rosita said softly. "Then you couldn't squeeze out again."

She lifted the top of the box. Curled up inside was HER kitten, furry white as she knew it would be.

When Rosita picked up the kitten, it stopped crying.

She knew it was hungry. "There's fish left over from last night," she told it.

Rosita forgot all about the eggs and bread. She also forgot about the landlord. She thought only about the kitten all the way home. When she walked into the apartment, Carlos cried, "No animals!"

"But it's lost, Carlos. It needs a home."

Carlos held the kitten and petted it. "It is pretty," he said, "but I'm sorry, Rosita, you can't keep it."

He touched the fur around the kitten's neck. "Even if you could have a pet, this kitten already has an owner. Didn't you see this tag?"

"If lost," Carlos read, "return to 38 King Street, Apartment 9. That's just around the corner from the grocery store," he said.

Carlos held out the kitten, and Rosita took it. It purred and sat back in her arms.

"Hurry now," said Carlos. "You must return the kitten."

Rosita did not move. Carlos turned her around and gently pushed her out the door.

As she walked, Rosita wondered about the people at 38 King Street.

"Are they unkind to you?" she asked the kitten. "Is that why you ran away?"

Rosita turned left at the corner on to King Street. She read the house numbers. Up ahead a house was boarded up, waiting to be taken down.

That's Number 38, she hoped. If the people had moved, she would HAVE to keep the kitten.

But no, Number 38 was next to the empty house. She opened the outside door and pushed the bell for Apartment 9.

"What is it?" A man stood on the stairs.

Rosita couldn't speak. She just held up the kitten.

"Maria!" the man shouted. "Quickly. Come!"

A sad-looking girl came out of an apartment. Then she saw Rosita and the kitten.

"Max," she shouted and ran downstairs. "Where did you find him? I've looked everywhere. Oh, Max, did you miss me?"

The man laughed. "Stop talking, Maria, and say thank you. I'm Mr. Petroni," he told Rosita.

Maria and Mr. Petroni asked so many questions. At last Rosita found her voice. She told them how she had found Max. She told them of wanting a pet and getting a plant.

"A plant for a pet," Maria said. "What a good idea! Can I come see it? Tomorrow morning? Then we can play with Max in the afternoon."

Rosita smiled all the way home. Playing with Max would be almost as good as keeping him, she thought. It was like having half a pet. And she had Maria to play with, too.

"Rosita! Watch out," Tony yelled.

She looked up just in time to catch the ball.

"Good catch," said Amy. "Want to play?"

Rosita nodded. "Tomorrow!" she said. "And can my friend play, too?"

I Wonder If Herbie's Home Yet

by Mildred Kantrowitz

Hello . . . Mr. Franklin?
This is Smokey.
Is Herbie home?
He went skating . . . with Lester?
LESTER PINKNEY?

No, no message, 'bye.
Boy that Herbie is one big fink!
That's a real friend.
A real NO-GOOD friend—that's what
Herbie is.
What good is Saturday if your
best friend's not around?
Lester Pinkney . . .
Lester Pinkney just happens to fall
over his feet all the time.
Lester Pinkney just happens to be
the smartest kid in the class.
I just don't happen to like
Lester Pinkney.

It couldn't be because of what happened
after school yesterday. Couldn't be.
I only said, "Herbie—you're asking
to borrow the only thing I ever wanted
in my life.
My birthday present.
It's not even scratched up yet.
Ask me anything else.
Ask me for anything else but my new,
red, high-rise banana bike."
He didn't ask me.

He just looked as I ran my hands
over those neat, silver handle bars.
Then he said, "So long, Smokey," and
walked away. He didn't seem to be mad.
We didn't have a fight or anything
like that.
All he said was, "So long, Smokey."
It's like saying, "See you tomorrow."
Only you don't have to SAY it.
If you're really good friends.
I'd give him anything else.
Anything else but my new red
banana bike.
Just last Saturday we were sitting
around, not doing anything.
I asked him what we should do—
and Herbie said, "Eat."
I said, "Like what?"
And he said, "Something sweet and cold."
So I got the dollar I had been saving
and we went down to CHARLIE'S.
We sat on the seats and ordered
the biggest ice-cream sundaes
you ever saw.

Then Herbie said, "OK if I pay you
tomorrow?"
And I said, "My treat."
"You, Smokey Silver," he said,
"are a great friend."
Then I said, "It's nothing. Forget it."
Well, he sure did!
How about the time he was going away
with his family for the weekend.
There was Herbie, standing outside
my front door that Friday night.

Herbie, with the gerbil, the dog,
the food, the cage, the bed.
He didn't have to ask. I knew.
So I said, "Sure, I'll take care
of them for you. What's
a best friend for?"
I said, "Herbie, you forgot to bring
over the top of the cage."
Herbie said, "He'll never make it
over the top.
He can't climb."

Well, he could. And he did.
Would you believe I spent most of that Saturday looking for the gerbil?
And that dumb dog!
That dumb, homesick dog kept barking and shaking—from loneliness, I guess.
I had to sleep in the basement with him to keep him quiet.
When Herbie came home, he said,
"I can never pay you back."
And I said, "It was nothing.
Forget it."
And he sure must have!!

I'll Show Herbie

I'll show Herbie.
I'll take all my old comic books
and set up my own stand and I'll take
the money and buy some potato chips
and soda pop.
I'll get all the kids over and
we'll have a party right here
on my front steps where Herbie
can see us and will HE be sorry!
Maybe there is a ball game
down at the park.
Maybe I'll "ump."
Maybe I'll catch.
Maybe I'll hit a home run.
Maybe Herbie will see me.
Herbie plays shortstop most
of the time.
I never told him, but you know—
he's a pretty rotten shortstop.
I never told him, because you don't
tell that to your best friend.
But now . . .

BUTTERFINGERS! Do you hear me, Herbie?
BUTTERFINGERS!

"Hello, Smokey. Home from the dentist so soon?"

I look up. Herbie's mother!

"Dentist," I say. "What dentist?"

"Why, Herbie said you had to go to the dentist this morning."

Oh, No!

I leave her standing there.
I take off and I'm running as fast as
I can down to the bottom of the hill.
Fifteen steps up.
RING THE BELL AND WALK IN.
So I do—right over to the lady
in white at the desk.
She knows I'm late.
I wish she wouldn't say it.
She nods her head—"You're late,"
she says.
She points to the one seat left.

"I forgot," I say, "Would you
believe it?"
She nods her head and points
to the seat again.
She never says much.
She just nods and points.
I sit and I wait and I wonder if
Herbie's home yet.
If I could call him, I'd say,
"Herbie, Lester Pinkney is ALL RIGHT!"
I'd say, "You're a great shortstop."
I'd say, "You've got a great brain.
You never forget anything!"
I'd say, "Herbie, you can borrow
my bike, any time you like.
And for as long as you want it."
And he'd say, "You're great."
And I'd say, "It's nothing. Forget it."
I wonder if Herbie's home yet . . .

Dictionary

mukluk 

harpoon 

tundra 

beluga 

caribou 

walrus 

Here is a picture dictionary. The words are in the wrong order. In what order do words go in a dictionary? Yes, they go in the order of the alphabet.

On a piece of paper, write the words in the right order. Here is an alphabet to help you:
ABCDEFGHIJKLMNOPQRSTUVWXYZ

Beluga is the first word.

Draw the pictures next to the words.

A.

Put on a Thinking Cap

M.

Think about the stories you just read.
Their names are listed below.
Now look at the pictures.
Tell which pictures go with each story.

B.

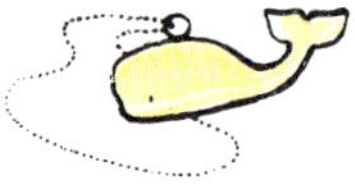

C.

Number a piece of paper from 1 to 4. Next to each number, write the letters of the pictures that go with that story. You may also want to draw the pictures that go with each story.

L.

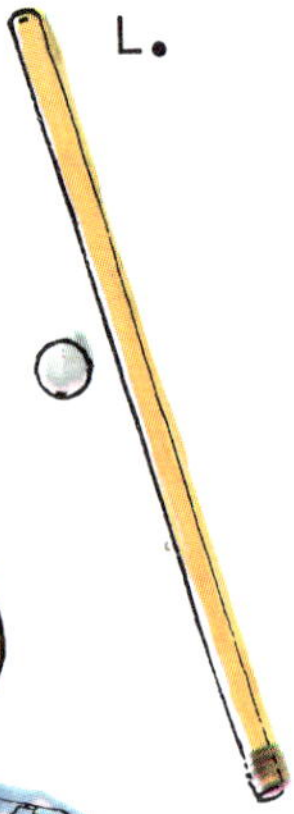

D.

J.

K.

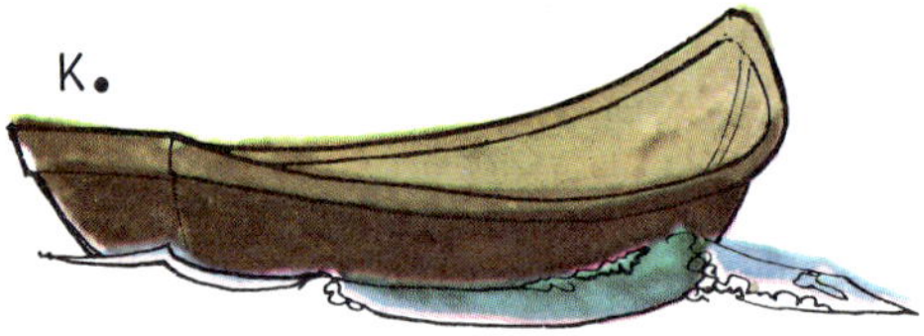

E.

1. The Dancing Class
2. Enuk, My Son
3. A Pet for Rosita
4. I Wonder If Herbie's Home Yet

I.

H.

F.

G.

Take Another Look

How the Brazilian Beetles Got Their Beautiful Coats

by Elsie Spicer Eells

In Brazil, the beetles have beautiful hard shelled coats upon their backs. Once upon a time, years and years ago, they had plain brown coats. This is the story of how the Brazilian beetle got a new coat.

One day a little brown beetle was crawling along a wall. A big gray rat ran out of a hole in the wall and looked down at the little beetle.

"How slowly you crawl along," he said to the beetle. "You will never get anywhere in the world. Just look at me and see how fast I can run."

The big gray rat ran to the end of the wall, turned around, and came back. The little beetle was slowly crawling along. She was

only a tiny way from where the rat had left her.

"Don't you wish that you could run like that?" said the big gray rat.

"You are a fast runner," said the little brown beetle. Her mother had told her always to be polite. She had told her that a polite beetle never boasts. So the little brown beetle never boasted one boast about the things SHE could do. She just went on slowly crawling along the wall.

A bright green and gold parrot in a mango tree heard them talking.

"How would you like to race with the beetle?" the parrot asked the big gray rat. "I will give a bright colored coat as a prize to the one who wins the race. You may have any color you like. I will have it made just the way you want."

"I would like a yellow coat with stripes like a tiger," said the big gray rat. He looked at his plain gray sides as if he were already seeing his new coat.

"I would like a beautiful, bright colored new coat, too," said the little brown beetle.

The big gray rat laughed long and loud until his plain gray sides were shaking. "Why, you talk just as if you thought you could win the race," he said.

The palm tree at the top of the hill would be the end of the race. The bright green and gold parrot gave the signal to start. Then he flew to the palm tree to watch for the end of the race.

The big gray rat ran as fast as he could. Then he thought how very tired he was getting. "What is the use of hurrying?" he said to himself. "The little brown beetle

cannot win. If I were racing with somebody who could really run, it would be very different."

So the big gray rat started to run slower, but his heart said, "Hurry up! Hurry up!" The big gray rat thought it was best to listen to the little voice in his heart. He hurried just as fast as he could.

Soon he reached the palm tree at the top of the hill. He could not believe his eyes. There was the little brown beetle sitting quietly beside the bright green and gold parrot. The big gray rat had never been so surprised in all his life.

"How did you run fast enough to get here before me?" he asked.

The little brown beetle showed the big gray rat the tiny wings under her hard shelled coat.

"Nobody said we had to run to win the race," she answered. "So I flew."

"I did not know that you could fly," said the big gray rat in a quiet little voice.

"Never judge anyone by looks alone," said the bright green and gold parrot to the big gray rat. "You never can tell where you may find hidden wings. You have lost the prize."

Then the parrot turned to the little brown beetle who was waiting quietly at his side.

"What color do you want your new coat to be?" he asked.

The little brown beetle looked up at the bright green and gold parrot and at the green and gold palm trees above their heads. She looked at the green mangoes with golden spots on their skins lying on the ground under the mango trees. She looked at the golden sunshine upon the far green hills. "I choose a coat of green and gold," she said.

From that day to this, the Brazilian beetle has worn a coat of green with gold spots on it. But to this day, the rat still wears a plain gray coat.

The Bear and the Butterfly

The bear and the butterfly had a fight
All of the day and most of the night,
Till at last the bear lay waving his paws
And the butterfly lit on one of his jaws.
Oh, never struggle and never fight
With a butterfly on a moonlight night!

—Margaret Wise Brown

The Way of an Ant

by Kazue Mizumura

Once there was a young ant who wanted to climb as high as the blue sky. He started to climb the tallest blade of grass he could find.

When he reached the top of the blade of grass, he looked up. He saw that a dandelion stood even higher.

He raced down to the ground and started to climb up the dandelion.

When he reached the top of the dandelion, he looked up. There, growing near the sky, he saw a rose. Its stem reached up as high as it could go.

He hurried to the ground and started to climb up the stem of the rose.

When he reached the rose, he stopped to smell its petals.

Then he thought he saw the sun in the sky. But it was only the gold ring of a sunflower. It was shining high above the rose.

He hurried down the stem of the rose to the ground. He started to climb up the sunflower.

When he reached the face of the sunflower, he looked up. The branch of an old apple tree with three green apples was above his head.

He quickly ran down to the ground and started to climb up the apple tree.

When he reached the top of the apple tree, he looked up. There was a maple tree shading him from the sky with its wide leaves.

He raced down to the ground and started to climb up the maple tree.

When he reached the top of the maple tree, he looked around for the blue sky. But there was a very large oak tree growing high over the field.

He ran down to the ground, hurried across the field, and started to climb up the oak tree.

When he reached the top of the oak tree, he was very, very tired. But the higher he climbed, the higher he wanted to climb.

Then he saw a pine tree on a faraway hilltop reaching up to the sky. He went down again to the ground, ran to the hilltop, and started to climb the pine tree.

When he reached the top of the pine tree, there was the blue sky as far as he could see. And there were hills and hills, and trees and trees as far as he could see. There were enough trees for him to climb forever.

At last he understood. As long as he went on climbing, the blue sky grew higher and higher.

He slowly turned his head and looked behind him.

There he saw the pine tree, the oak tree, the maple tree, the apple tree, the sunflower, the rose, the dandelion, and the grass.

How surprised he was to see how hard he had tried. How happy he was to have climbed so high.

But now he was much older and a little wiser. He would climb no more.

He started down the pine tree. On the way, he met a young ant hurrying to climb up to the sky.

The old ant smiled and nodded at the young ant, and went by without saying a word.

In a Few Words

TOO BAD! The firefly seen by daylight
Is only a bug with a red neck.

—*Bashō*

We caught
some stars
last night
and got our feet wet.
The fields were full of fireflies.

—*Ronni Solbert*

Rachel Carson: A Woman Who Changed Our World

by Judith Adams

Did you know that a book could change the world? Rachel Carson wrote a book that did!

Rachel called her book *Silent Spring.* It begins with the story of a make-believe town. Birds were everywhere. People came from far and wide to watch the birds. They watched them fly south in winter. They watched them fly north in summer.

Fish swam in the cool, clear streams. Fruit trees bloomed in the green fields.

In the fall, the trees in the woods turned bright red and gold.

But something happened to the town. When spring came, the trees were without leaves. There were no fish in the streams. There were no birds filling the air with their music.

Here and there, the homes were dusted with a white powder. It was the deadly poison, DDT. The DDT was used to kill harmful insects. But DDT had killed more than insects—it had killed the animals, fish, and birds all around the countryside.

Rachel Carson wrote about this make-believe town

for a reason. She wanted to show what would happen if people kept using poisons like DDT.

Rachel also told about the REAL harm DDT had already done. She told about one American town where beetles were killing the elm trees. DDT was used on the elms, and soon the beetles died. But so did all the robins around. Why? Because worms ate the elm leaves dusted with DDT. Then the robins ate the poisoned worms. DDT had gone from the leaf to the worm to the bird!

DDT had killed animals, birds, and insects in many other places, too. Rachel Carson knew that all living things share the earth. She believed people should care for all life, not just for themselves. She wrote that poisons like DDT could hurt this "web of life" for good.

Silent Spring made people very angry. Some of them were angry at Rachel Carson! These people wanted to go on using DDT. They would not believe what she said about DDT.

Other people were angry because they believed what Rachel Carson said. They didn't want DDT to be used again anywhere.

The fighting over DDT went on for 10 years. Then, in 1972, the use of DDT was stopped once and for all. Rachel Carson's book had helped to change things—for the better.

Who was Rachel Carson? How did she come to write *Silent Spring*? Rachel had always cared about nature—ever since she was a little girl living in the country. When she grew up, Rachel became a scientist. She worked for the United States Bureau of Fisheries for many years. There she gathered facts about the fish in American waters.

Rachel was also a writer. All of her books were about nature. One of the things she liked best was the sea. How wonderful the sea was! Rachel wrote about the ocean winds and the underwater mountains. She wrote about the birds that live on the shore, the fish that live in the open sea, and eels that live on the sea floor.

Before writing a book, Rachel found out all she could about the creatures that would be in it. She spent a long time in icy waters looking for many

of the animals she wrote about. Rachel wanted to see them up close. There was the barnacle with its feather-like feet. And the blue-eyed scallop, with its two rows of eyes—about forty of them!

Often, Rachel watched these sea animals until late at night. Then, even if she was very tired, she didn't rest until she put them back where she found them.

Sometimes Rachel explored nature with her nephew. At night they went out to find crabs on the shore. There they would smell the seaweed and the fish. Sometimes they looked in the grass for night insects.

In the day time, they often walked in the woods after a rain. The plants looked beautiful when they were wet!

Rachel wrote about their walks. She said that everyone can enjoy nature—even city people. Look up at the white clouds during the day. See the silvery stars at night. Listen to the wind as it whistles past a tall building. Feel the rain. Go to a park and watch the birds flying past. Plant a seed and see it grow. Look at the trees and plants each day, as if you had never seen them before!

Rachel did not like to think that people were harming the "web of life." But she saw what was happening with her own eyes. The air was full of car fumes. Rivers were dirty. People were using poisons that were killing not only harmful insects but also harmless animals.

Didn't people know that they shared the earth with all the other living creatures? Didn't they know that every living thing needs every other living thing? Learning about this need to share the earth is called *ecology*. Rachel wanted people to understand what ecology means.

Today, many people do know what ecology means. Many people care about all life and want to protect it. We have Rachel Carson to thank for this.

Did You Know . . . ?

Here are some words that are alike in one way. Can you tell what it is?

Each one is made of two words put together. Can you find the two words in each one?

Words made up of two words put together are called compound words. Look at the little words in each compound word. What does each little word mean? What does each compound word mean?

There are a number of compound words in this unit. See how many you can find. Write them on paper. Tell a friend what each of your compound words means.

Take a Good Look

Look closely at the pictures below.
Some of the things are very much alike.

Do you know which things are alike?
How are they alike? How many groups
of things that are alike can you find?

You should have found three groups
of things that are alike—fish, birds, and plants.

Now take a piece of paper. Draw
two more birds, two fish, and two plants.

WORD LIST

Included in this list are all words used in *Moon Magic* which have not appeared in earlier levels of PATHFINDER—Allyn and Bacon Reading Program.

The words are listed in the order of their introduction in each story. The number at the left indicates the page on which a word first appears.

The words are classified into three types:

Foundation Words: Words which will appear repeatedly in the program. These are the foundation of the children's reading vocabulary and are given special emphasis in instruction.

Skill-based Words: Words which most children should be able to read independently by applying decoding skills taught either in earlier lessons at this level or at previous levels. Skill-based words in this list are printed in **boldface** type.

Story-specific Words: Words which are important to the understanding of a particular selection but which are not systematically maintained or reused at this level. Many of these words will recur in pupils' recreational reading and most will be in the listening and speaking vocabularies of most of the children. Story-specific words in this list are printed in *italics.*

Variant forms of previously introduced words are not considered new to the program if the generalization for forming the variant has been taught. Also not considered new are compounds formed from known parts, contractions formed from known parts using previously learned generalizations, and words which are parts of previously learned compounds.

4. *rabbit*
India
sure
years
anyone
else
before
woods

5. *hunt*
catch

6. *fruit*
brought
gone

7. **rock**
burning
meat

8. caught
hands
really
Indra
king
yourself
shall
sky
moon
spots

10. *mouse*
Arthur
enough
watch
cool

11. felt
nose
whiskers
only
yellow
eyes
light
cheese

12. **tonight**
thought
farther
edge
meadow

corn field
golden
wheat
misty
set
past

13. **stars**

14. **steps**

15. *nibbled*

16. *soft*
cloudy

17. *clouds*
thin
slice
whole

18. *Squaps*
moonling
astronaut
landed
beings
air
stone
wrote
dust
interested
pair

19. **stems**
finished

20. *welcome*
leg
person
left

21. *remembered*
seen
enjoy
Tom
Brigitte
covered

22. *excited*
necklace
Squaps-pff-krr
understand
joy

23. never
done
cloth
squeezed

24. *shower*
bath
grass
hose
through

25. *cheer*
chairs
hung

26. *eight*
o'clock
strange
wrong
floating

27. **fly**

28. **bring**
suit
believe

34. *chest*
ribs
lungs
mouth
breath

35. *throat*
ahhhhhhhhh
fingers

36. *larynx*
voice
neck
both
slit

37. *mirror*
curl
lips
teeth
tongue
tap

38. **hum**
ma-ah-ah-ah
me-ee-ee-ee
moo-oo-oo-oo

39. **beans**
bananas

41. *Sia*
Kilimanjaro
Africa
does
snow
coffee
bushes

42. *Sariko*
hut
straw
windows
Chagga
already
knife
Linga
six

43. *carry*
Saika
Kitutu
feast
Moshi
Marealle

44. *Mamole*
young

45. *chiefs*
behind

46. *forest*
Kifura
bunch
pole
starts
tiny

47. **driver**
road

48. *though*
loud
frightened

49. **also**
speak

50. *points*
dreaming
spoken
cross

54. *truth*
Mylo
answering
finally

55. *robbers*
suppose
ghosts
explain
habits
customs
worried
disappoint
either
able
bought
package
modeling
clay

56. first
lumps
thumb
prints
statue

57. *realize*
artistic
busy
reason
figure
exactly

58. suddenly
perfect

proud
special
matter

59. *wandering*
wild
sort

61. **woke**
afterward

62. *thief*
hall
Lucky
Jasmine
grabbed

63. *Mai Ling*
parents
vacuum
Wednesday
rule
dirt
knocked
Peggy

64. **doll**
course
yesterday

65. afternoon

66. **bowl**

67. *purse*
phone
rang
turned

68. *fork*
garbage
stomach
Chinese
dragon

69. *bury*
bent

70. **dug**
tossed
hurried
second

72. tail
stairs
sorry

73. *whispered*
ho dor jeh

74. *birthday*
Suzie
bicycle
knee
scrape
hurt

75. *two wheeler*
Clem
barn

76. *grandmother*
canning

78. **kickstand**
pedal
ready

79. *meter*

83. *cheeseburger*

90. **Salem**
Massachusetts
toys
puppets
arms
blocks
drums
early
Americans
Robert
Richard
Rebecca

91. **England**
pears
peaches
cherries

92. **dishes**
tools
shop

93. *captain*
Nicholas
square
brace
sandpaper
smooth
cherry

95. *candlesticks*
packing
pillow

97. **dress**
Isabel

98. *great-great-grandfather*

100. **hammer**
board
steel
bang
bar
soap

101. **heavy**
carpenter

102. *claw*
sledge

103. **drummer**
break

104. *handles*
break
act
nuts
arrow head

105. **brick**
crash
sends

106. across
mallets
croquet

107. **baseball**
music
xylophone
piano

108. *keys*

109. **judge**
order
gavel

110. **pancakes**
cock-a-doodle-doo
rooster
breakfast
flour

111. *mill*
rode
donkey's

112. *grain*
shorter
beat

113. **pocket**
cluck

115. **pail**
stool

116. *butter*
churn

117. *logs*

118. *sweet*
jelly
maple
syrup
strawberry

119. **mixing**
pour
batter

melted

120. *minute*
flip

121. *yummmm*

124. *city*
brushes

125. **cone**
tastes

126. *diesel*
shovels
dump
country
tractors
plows
wagons
reapers
crops

127. **plows**
trailers
campers

128. **zoom**
track
ambulances
hospital

129. **own**

130. *airplanes*
airports

136. *Jacques*
Cousteau
pioneer
important
born
France

137. *explore*
oceans

138. *probably*
Aqua-lung
divers
breathe

139. *camera*
sunken
diving saucer

140. *worms*
sharks

141. *telephones*

142. *swum*
turtles
whales

143. *sank*
movies
television

144. **means**
rivers
pollution
killed

146. *island*
goddess
Japan
often

147. **maidens**
listen
song
rises

148. *storm*
thunder
lightning
shore

150. *changing*

151. **which**

152. *Loch Ness*
Scotland
body

154. *earthquake*
blocked

155. *plesiosaur*
flippers

156. *echo sounder*
radar

157. *humps*

158. *visiting*

159. *joking*
barrels
metal

160. *footprints*
hippopotamus

166. *Angela's*
lessons
community
center
since
wore

167. *Saturday*

168. **coat**
wearing
tights

169. stood
straight
practicing
Charleen
exercises

170. **lie**
forth

171. *positions*
bend
plié

172. **lifting**
leap
corner

174. *Enuk*
son
honk
north
Eskimos
Tigara
whale

175. **sod**
during
muktuk
skin
favorite
village
umelik
mukluks
fur
boots
pants
walrus
stitches
frame

176. *spout*
tent
clothes
sled
team

177. *several*
harpoon
fed

178. *threw*
cold
silent

179. **tea**
ivory
charm

180. *poked*
sharply
paddle

181. *fear*
backward
shot

splashing

182. *splishhhhhh*
beluga
puffing
dragging
struggled
blood
dead

184. *Nalukatuk*
fried
doughnuts
oil

185. *aie*
swung

187. *Rosita*
pitch

188. *curb*
litter
basket
Carlos
present
Mexico

189. *landlord's*
Perez
cities

190. *guess*
sheet

192. **instead**
kissed
sent

193. *above*
below

194. *grocery*

196. **tag**
purred

197. *gently*
unkind
numbers
empty

198. *Maria*

199. *Petroni*
questions

200. *half*

201. **nodded**

202. **Franklin**
Smokey
Herbie
Lester
Pinkney

203. **message**
smartest

204. *borrow*
scratched

205. **neat**
silver
fight
dollar
saving
Charlie's
sundaes

206. *treat*
Friday

207. *gerbil*

208. *spent*
loneliness
basement

209. **comic**
buy
potato
chips
soda
pop
ump
rotten

210. *butterfingers*
dentist

211. **fifteen**
ring
desk

212. **brain**

216. *Brazilian*
beetles
Brazil
hard shelled
upon
ago
plain
crawling

217. **polite**
boasts

218. **gold**
parrot
mango
stripes

219. *palm*
signal

220. *heart*
beside
wings

222. **lying**
choose
worn

224. *blade*
dandelion

225. **stem**
petals

226. *branch*
shading

227. *oak*

229. **wiser**

231. *Rachel*
Carson

232. *south*
clear
streams

233. *powder*
poison
harmful
insects

234. **died**
robins
leaf

235. **web**

236. *nature*
became
bureau
gathered
ocean
eels
creatures

237. *barnacle*
scallop
forty

238. *nephew*
crabs
seaweed

240. *fumes*
harmless

241. *ecology*
protect

DPT

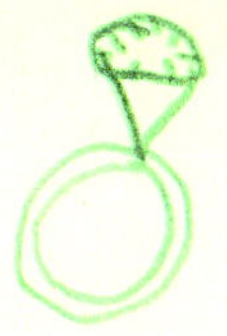

Ring